# DON'T ASK AND I WILL TELL

## Finding Myself in Vietnam

NEW HANOVER COUNTY PUBLIC LIBRARY
201 Chestnut Street
Wilmington, N.C. 28401

John Carroll Whitener, Lt. Col. USAR (Ret.)

D1545906

Tim O'Brien excerpt from *The Things They Carried* Copyright 1990 by Houghton Mifflin Harcourt. Reprinted with the permission from Houghton Mifflin Harcourt.

Happy Valley Press
Asheville, N.C.
Copyright 2017 by John Carroll Whitener

ISBN-13 978-0692862414
ISBN-10 0692862412

Library of Congress Cataloging–in-Publication Data
LCCN: 2017904073

BISAC Biography & Autobiography/ Personal Memoir

Subjects: Vietnam, 101st Airborne Division, military, sexuality, gay man, gay soldier, spiritual journey, Christian, memoir

This book can be purchased in bulk for promotional or educational purposes. Please contact your local bookseller or Happy Valley Press by e-mail at HappyValleyPress@gmail.com.

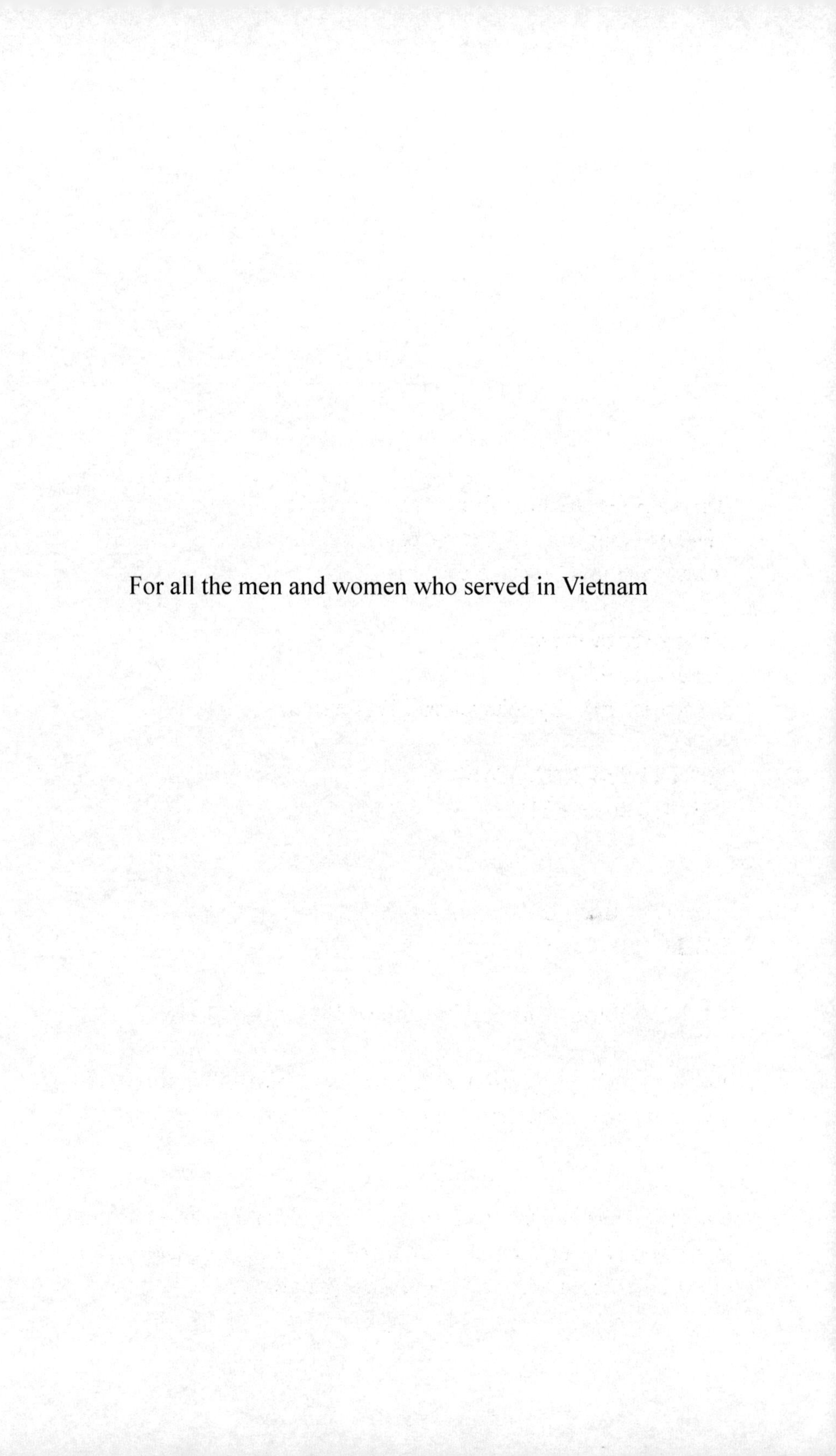

For all the men and women who served in Vietnam

Stories are for those late hours in the night when you can't remember how you got from where you were to where you are. Stories are for eternity, when memory is erased, when there is nothing to remember except the story.

Tim O'Brien, author of *The Things They Carried*

Scientists tell us we are made of atoms, but I say we are made of stories.

Quote from Eduardo Galeano in TV interview,
author of *Open Veins of Latin America*

# CONTENTS

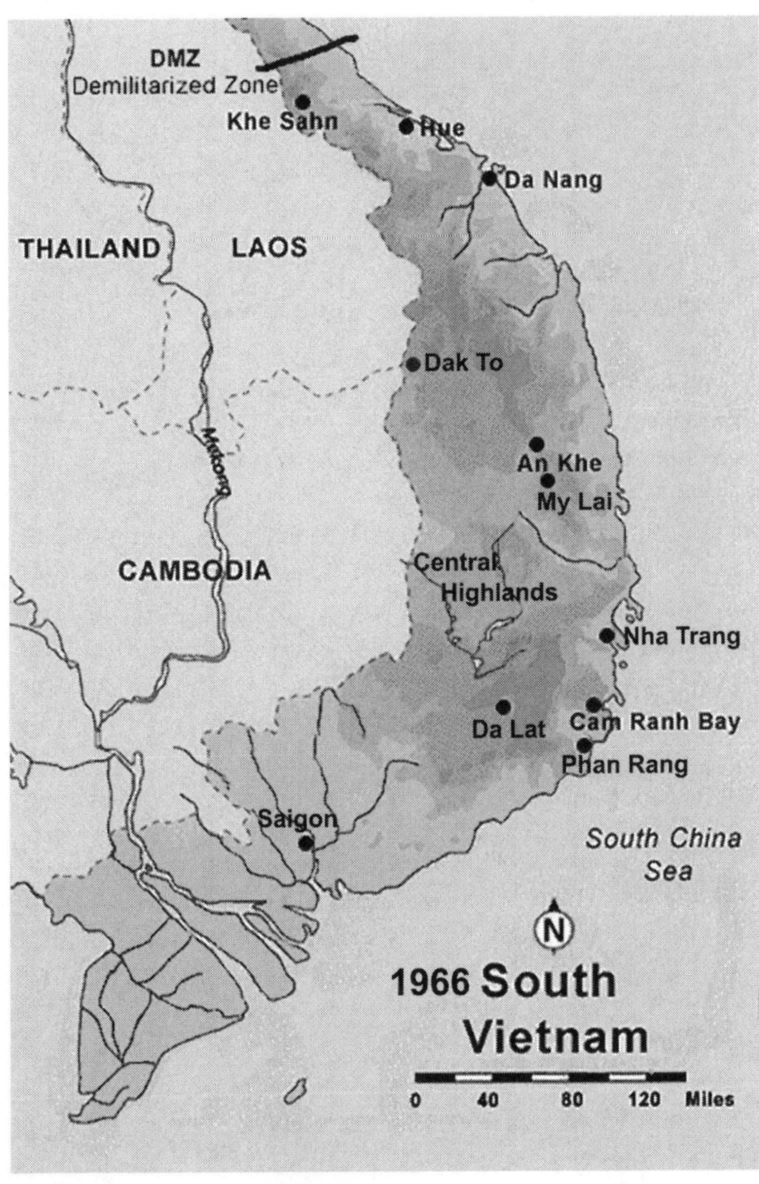


| | |
|---|---|
| **Phan Rang:** | 221st Medical Detachment assigned to 101st Airborne Division Base Camp |
| **Cam Ranh Bay:** | 1st Logistical Command<br>61st Medical Battalion Headquarters |
| **Nha Trang:** | 43rd Medical Group and 8th Field Hospital |

# INTRODUCTION

Singer Rufus Wainwright said, "A person is born twice. First, at birth, and then again, when his mother dies." In John 3:4, Nicodemus asks Jesus, "How can someone be born when they are old?"

Recently I've stumbled upon my own answer to that question. Both of my parents died within a year. Two months after Mother died, I retired from the job I'd held for thirty-four years. It was a time for my rebirth.

I have had a rich and full life. I have known love; I have excelled in my career; I have enjoyed countless friendships. Yes, I have made mistakes, and unlike the young Mick Jagger, I don't feel that "Time is on my side." I like to imagine that I might have ten more good years. But then, maybe not.

Like most people who experience the deaths of family and friends, I have acknowledged my own mortality. I am evaluating what things in life are really important. I am trying to be less judgmental about people and events, and in the process, learning to accept myself. I've come to realize that we are all complex individuals, and we are all children of God.

And so as a child of God, a unique being, and a man who has come to grips with being gay, Christian, a soldier, and the mutability of all things, I set out to write this memoir about my year in Vietnam.

For many years I repressed the emotional and psychological ramifications of being a Christian and a closeted gay soldier. The constant secrecy weighed on my consciousness, whether in uniform or not. If the military didn't kick me out for sexual misconduct, the majority of states could have charged me with a crime. In my home state of North Carolina, homosexual activity was cruelly named the "crime against nature."

Memories can be tricky, especially those buried and decayed over a lifetime. It's easy to rewrite history to suit an image I want to project. Fortunately, I don't have to rely solely on my memory. When I was a young soldier in Vietnam, I kept a diary from July of 1966 to July of 1967, and recently I read it for the first time. Although I recorded given names in the diary, I have changed some of the names in the stories with the privacy of my colleagues in mind.

In each chapter I begin with an italicized diary entry, followed by my current reflection on the story. I hope the events chronicled, and the commentary, will provide some understanding about the daily life of soldiers in a base camp in Vietnam, as well as insight about the challenges of rectifying religion and sexuality. Perhaps some things should remain unsaid, but the events provide illumination for a specific time and place, which shaped me into the person I am. Vietnam forever changed the trajectory of my life.

Several times in my account I state that I was "lucky." Upon further reflection, I believe that my tour in Vietnam and my experiences throughout my life have been possible, not only by good luck, but by God's love and grace.

# ALL THE WAY

***21 June 1967***

*Each battalion of 101st Airborne Division has a different salutation, which the soldiers shout out as they salute an officer. Here are some of the greetings: "Above the rest, sir," "Second to none, sir," "Can do, sir," and "Strike force, sir." One of my favorites is "All the way, sir."*

*As he returned salutes, a new major in the 1st Log Battalion came back with a new greeting: "Zero defects."*

*Brilliant! My mental retort is "Peace."*

*I don't have my orders to return to the States, and I'm on the brink of losing my sanity. I can't sit still long enough to read a book. Time seems endless, and sleep is my respite from boredom. I go to bed early in the evening, but it's no fun alone. The next roommate I have will definitely be female.*

*This week I received a letter from a minister in North Carolina. He knows my parents, who told him about my work with youth in the church. He stated in the letter that he is looking forward to meeting me when I return. Although I don't know him, the letter was very personable.*

Why would I seek a female roommate? I liked women as friends, but in my heart of hearts I knew I could never marry one. I wanted to love a man, but my religious upbringing and the laws of the land made that choice seem impossible.

When I returned to the States, I met the charismatic letter-writing minister, whom I will call Victor, on a weekend visit to my parents. He was pastor of my former church, married with children. He and his wife were also close friends of my parents, spending the previous Christmas at our family gatherings.

I attended a Sunday service, in which he preached to the *Christians* to get right with God. I was not surprised, because church teachings make most everything a sin, which requires repentance during the altar call. The prolonged call included a hymn of guilt ("Almost persuaded…sad, sad that bitter wail, almost, but lost!") while the minister pleaded to sinners to confess or to Christians to make a new commitment.

Victor was sycophantic. In casual conversation on one of my subsequent visits to my parents, Victor learned that I was furnishing my apartment and couldn't find a floor-length, round tablecloth. He offered to sew a tablecloth with material of my choice. I accepted and bought brown faux-alligator oilcloth with orange and beige fringe on the bottom. In retrospect, the tablecloth screamed gay.

And then the phone calls began. Although I had given Victor no reason to think I was romantically interested in him, he professed that he was in love with me. I stopped answering the phone.

One weekend on my way to visit my parents, Victor saw my car pass his house and followed me until I stopped. He got out of his car, and I rolled down my window. He said, "I'm in love with you."

With my heart pounding so hard I thought it would explode, I mustered up enough courage to reply, "I can't handle it. Stop calling me."

"Please don't tell anyone," he said.

"O.K. Of course I won't."

I never discussed my sexuality with anyone, and certainly not with an evangelical minister, who preached in a fundamentalist church. At that time there were no ministers or teachers to offer positive information or counseling about homosexuality. No movies or TV shows with openly gay actors. No role models, textbooks, few novels (the main characters were unhappy and suicidal). No solace.

I had suppressed my homosexual desires all my life and prayed for God to change me. Confronting the minister was a transformational event that freed me to explore, albeit carefully, my desire for men. The teachings of my church, which had condemned me, could no longer control my life.

Though I never accepted Victor's offer, the minister helped me realize that even in the church, anyone can be homosexual. His declaration forced me to confront my biggest fear and my greatest fantasy: the love of another man. I was not all the way out of the closet, but the door was cracking open.

Meanwhile, I was still in the Army.

# FLASHBACK

***9 July 1966***

*As I write, the ocean waves are slapping the ship and rocking me into a state of hypnosis. I am in my bunk bed in a ten by twelve foot cabin shared with three other officers. Two bunk beds are stacked on each side of the room. I chose a bottom bunk...*

1966 was the year for my first ship cruise—and many first-time experiences. Looking back, I recognize that is was the year I seriously questioned my values, my faith—and my sexuality.

My journey began almost two years earlier, in October 1964, when I entered the U.S. Army's Medical Service Corps. The military had begun drafting optometrists, especially those who were newly graduated. I had passed the North Carolina State Board, and with my newly acquired optometry degree in hand I was ready to set up practice in my home town, but I didn't want to do so only to be drafted. Also, I wanted to choose my own duty station. So instead of waiting to be called up, I volunteered. One way or the other, I accepted my fate.

I still remember vividly my military induction physical in Southside Chicago during my final year at Illinois College of Optometry. I think

I was the only white guy taking the physical. Even then, all signs pointed to the fact that more African-American men would serve in Vietnam than in any other American war. (Sadly, 14 percent of Americans who died in the Vietnam War were black soldiers, while they made up 11 percent of the young male population nationwide.)

Compared to the dark, muscular men that I covertly surveyed in the room, I had a real inferiority complex about my own pale, skinny body. When we all dropped our drawers for the hernia check, I heard the other men snickering. I nervously glanced at the many well-endowed young men. Did my body amuse them?

I survived the physical, but to complete the medical history form, I confronted a moral and life-changing dilemma: "Do you have homosexual tendencies?"

Because the military defined homosexuality as a mental illness, I could have told the truth, checked "Yes," and come away with a 4F classification—"undesirable/unfit for military duty." I could have avoided military duty altogether.

But I knew that the consequences of a 4F classification might drastically affect my optometric career. In North Carolina, where I was licensed to practice, a doctor could be suspended for "moral turpitude," meaning conduct considered contrary to community standards of good morals. This crime, which could deprive me of a livelihood, evolved from England's ecclesiastical laws relating to human flaw, or falling from grace.

Certainly, I was afraid of admitting homosexual tendencies, but even more, I could not reconcile the idea of falling from God's grace. Nor could I handle telling my parents, for I was certain the consequences would be devastating.

I had been taught never to tell a lie…

I lied.

I checked "No," and headed to basic training at Fort Sam Houston, Texas.

Unlike me, a lot of the trainees had previous military experience through the Reserve Officers' Training Corps. (I had received my commission based solely on the fact that I held a Doctor of Optometry degree.)

I had never fired a rifle. I had never been camping or ever slept in a tent. I was so embarrassed by my laughable marching in formation that I asked a fellow trainee to help me practice the marching commands and steps in the evenings in the parking lot of the Bachelor Officer Quarters.

By some miracle I passed basic training, including target qualifying with the M14 rifle and the .45 caliber pistol, which was the standard-issue sidearm for medical officers. I was ready—at least according to the U.S. Army—to defend my patients and myself in time of war. So, after six weeks of training at Fort Sam Houston, I received orders for my first duty station: Ireland Army Hospital.

Ireland! I had no idea the U.S. had armed forces stationed in Ireland. I had requested Europe as my first choice of duty stations, and now I was on my way—a dream come true.

Then I reread the first paragraph of my orders.

Apparently Ireland Army Hospital was not located in Ireland, but in Fort Knox, Kentucky—the first of many realities that did not match my naive expectations.

Okay, I can live with this fate, I thought. I would stay in the army for three years at Fort Knox, complete my military duty, and return to Hickory, North Carolina. There I would set up my own practice, marry the woman of my dreams, and live happily ever after.

Fort Knox provided basic training for newly inducted soldiers, and thanks to the military draft and the buildup of American soldiers in Vietnam, hundreds of soldiers lined for eye exams. Each day as I weaved my way through the queue to get to the front door of my clinic, I was astounded with the number of patients. During my fourteen months at Fort Knox, I had over five thousand patient encounters.

Free time was sparse, but at the Fort Knox Little Theatre I honed my insufferable acting skills in three plays: First, a forgettable French farce in which I played the innocent young man who was taken advantage of by the maid. (This role didn't require acting: I played myself.) In *A Thousand Clowns* I had to act straight as the brother/uncle. To my chagrin, I didn't get the starring role of Doc, the recovering alcoholic chiropractor in William Inge's *Come Back, Little Sheba*; I played the non-speaking role of the postman. In some way my amateur acting days prepared me for a more serious role as a straight soldier.

Suddenly, life changed. I received orders for "a classified area overseas." I had learned my lesson, so I knew the classified area was not Ireland.

I was going to Vietnam.

To prepare me for the inevitable, my friends gave me a surprise going-away party. The DJ called the music "disco." I was raised in the Church of God, so just like playing cards, going to movies, and of course, sex before marriage, dancing was a sin. Nevertheless, I sinned. Boldly. I moved my body to the pulsating music, and I liked it.

The next day I flew home to Hickory for a week. It was an emotionally difficult time for my mother, who feared for my safety. I was the first child, and we had established an exclusive bond for seven years before the birth of my first brother. I tried to reassure my parents that I would be safe with God watching over me. In late May 1966, I said goodbye to my parents and boarded a plane to Seattle. My mother promised to write every day while I was in Vietnam, and she did.

I don't recall being afraid of dying. After all, I was a doctor, not an infantryman. What I was afraid of was my attraction to men. I didn't know how I would cope with the lack of privacy while living in a shared tent. Would I be kicked out of the Army for my homosexual tendencies?

My new unit, the 221st Medical Dispensary, formed at Fort Lewis, Washington—the same army post where Daddy had been a medical corpsman during the Second World War. I joined the newly formed dispensary staff, which consisted of Marv Youkilis, Gene Fishman, and George Schnetzer, physicians; Jim Mahoney, dentist; Ron Walker, administrative officer; and seventeen medical corpsmen. I filled the optometrist slot. We were there for several weeks while ordering and packing equipment for use in our dispensary in Vietnam.

I had free time on weekends, so one weekend I went to Seattle, where I took a date to dinner in the revolving restaurant on the top floor of the Space Needle. The view of the Puget Sound and Mount Rainer, nearly fifty miles away, was breathtaking. My date was a nurse whom I knew when she was stationed at Fort Knox. (Try as I might, I can't remember her name.) Although I told the guys in our unit she was a date, she was just a female friend. I dated women to keep up the appearance, and to convince myself, that I could be heterosexual. I remember no goodbye kiss—only the spectacular view from the Space Needle—and no further effort to keep in touch.

On another weekend, I took the opportunity to visit Mrs. Macintyre, a friend of my parents still living in Tacoma. Daddy frequently told the story about meeting the Macintyres for the first time for Thanksgiving dinner in 1944. He had assumed that "dinner" meant eating the midday meal: Growing up in the South, the noon meal was referred to as dinner and the evening meal was supper. He and his buddy, another soldier, were hungry and ready to eat when Mrs. Macintyre picked them up from Fort Lewis in late morning. To his chagrin, Thanksgiving dinner was not served until five that evening. Mrs. Macintyre's generosity continued when she offered to rent Daddy a small, tar-papered house—a former garage—on her property. The Thanksgiving Day celebration was the beginning of a lifetime friendship with the Macintyre family.

My mother and I had been living in Hickory till that point, and now, with a place for us to live, Daddy asked us to join him. A combination of love for my Daddy and concern about my health helped Mother make a decision. She had taken me to Dr. Frye to find out why I wouldn't eat. He said either I was too lazy to eat (unbelievable) or I was pining for my Daddy. She believed the latter. I am in awe of the courage of my mother, which enabled her to pack a suitcase and travel 2,700 miles with me via trains from Hickory to Tacoma, Washington. The national polio epidemic complicated our departure. Hickory had the most polio cases in North Carolina, and a quarantine required her to obtain a letter from the same doctor stating that I didn't have polio.

My mother had never traveled without Daddy. Mother told me that she was frequently met with kindness from strangers during the five-day journey. Soldiers traveling on the crowded trains stood up and gave her their seats.

Mother worked at the Fort Lewis post office, which she described as the best job of her life. When she returned to Hickory after the war, she might have worked in the local post office but instead she found a job in the hosiery mill. Years later she stayed at home inspecting socks, which Daddy brought home each evening in huge canvas bags. The memory of that small, dank cellar with a single fluorescent fixture to light her inspection board is haunting, but inspecting socks enabled Mother to remain at home and earn money to help make ends meet. She was there when my siblings and I left for school, and when we returned in the afternoon greeted with the aroma of supper cooking.

On July 7, 1966, our dispensary personnel flew from Seattle to Oakland, California. We were among the 10 percent of the military who traveled to Vietnam via ship from California. We docked briefly in San Diego to pick up two thousand Marines.

In an effort to boost morale, a Special Services staffer had arranged for two local strippers, Frosty and Firecracker, to come down to the dock to take off their clothes for God and Country. At twenty-four years old, I had never been in a bar or strip joint. I foolishly wondered if the ship would tip over, since every soldier and sailor on board rushed to the side of the ship facing the strippers. The only detail I remember was from the neck up: Frosty had bleached blond hair, and Firecracker's was bright red.

And—well, yes—tassels whirled in every direction, impressing the bedazzled troops.

Frosty and Firecracker took a final bow, and off we went (so to speak) on our cruise on the USNS General W. H. Gordon, a twenty-year-old troop transport ship. The enlisted men ate and slept on the lower deck, in cavernous open bays with no windows and no privacy. Their bunks—consisting of canvas stretched tightly on metal frames supporting a mattress, sheets, a blanket, and a pillow—were stacked three high with about two feet of space between them. One week out to sea the air-conditioning system broke, which made life miserable in the bowels of the ship.

For the enlisted men, food was served cafeteria-style. Since I was a privileged officer, dining was a much better experience. We were served seated at round tables (eight to a table) with tablecloths, and we were given choices for the entrée.

If you played bridge (I didn't), you had other companions to help stave off boredom. A group of black soldiers organized a one-time talent show in which they choreographed and sang "My Girl," made famous by the Temptations the previous year. In my sheltered musical world of Pat Boone and hymnody, I had never listened to Smokey Robinson and Motown music.

For three weeks, thousands of young, testosterone-filled troops were confined to the ship with nothing to do. I admit that I had my own testosterone issues and found a few men attractive, including one who was in my Bible study. But fear of being outed, as well as prayer, overrode my desire to pursue sexual feelings.

Idleness gave rise to rumors. Without a cell phone or the Internet, it was difficult to separate speculation from fact. Most of the rumors were war stories, but I remember a particular unbelievable story about the systematic slaughter of eight student nurses in South Chicago. The story was that a young man broke into an apartment building, and over a period of hours, stabbed or strangled eight nurses after leading them into a room one-by-one, and raping the last victim. Of course, the hideous story was not a rumor, and the killer was Richard Speck.

The monotonous, prosaic routine was the same most days: rise at 0730, shave and dress in military fatigues by 0800, breakfast at 0815, Bible study at 1000, lunch at 1215, nap at 1330, read a book at 1400, enjoy the sea breeze at 1600, supper at 1715, walk around the deck, shoot the breeze with colleagues after supper, listen to the radio at 1900, write in my journal at 2100, and then lights out.

Life on the ship was boring, but the routine proved helpful, because I carved out time to write in my journal.

***9 July 1967 (continued)***
*Tonight I tuned in to Radio Moscow. The program—in perfect English—was called "Vietnam Flashback."*

It was obvious propaganda from the left and reminded me of statements from Senators Wayne Morse (OR) and Ernest Greuning (AK), condemning our actions in Vietnam. They were the only senators to oppose the 1964 Gulf of Tonkin Resolution, which authorized the president to take military action in Southeast Asia without a declaration of war.

The keyword from Moscow was "aggression," which was repeated in almost every sentence. A sampling of world opinion from leaders of Mexico, Italy, Germany, and other countries condemned U.S. aggression and U.S. bombings in Vietnam. An unnamed English professor from Hanoi gave his eyewitness account of cruelties to the people of Vietnam by the American forces:

"Gas has been used by Americans to kill women, children, and old people," he said. "I can't understand how a country of plenty that represents goodwill to impoverished people could destroy so much in Vietnam."

Then a "newsflash" reported that an entire Special Forces camp had been wiped out five miles from Saigon. It didn't sound possible, but who can tell reality from propaganda when both sides manage the news? Who can understand war? The program concluded with beautiful classical music and the announcer inviting his listeners to stay tuned at the same time, same station for more.

Afterwards, as I walked out on the deck and scanned the horizon, I was overwhelmed by the vastness of the cerulean sea. The only sound I heard was the rolling swells of the Pacific slapping against the ship's hull. A sense of peace flooded my soul, and I felt close to God.

But that sentiment would change.

# CAM RANH BAY

***31 July 1966***

*A choppy ocean caused the U.S.N.S. Gordon to sway as we approached the shore. While plumes of black smoke rose from the distant mountains, overhead multiple fighter jets roared. My senses were on overload. War was not far away.*

*After 23 days on board, I waited anxiously for a small boat to take us ashore at Cam Ranh Bay. The confinement on the ship was overwhelming. How do prisoners live in confinement for years? The vacation from normal duties was fun, but I was ready to begin work.*

*I was amazed at how good it felt to walk on land again. The Army engineers had already set up our camp several miles inland. Our sleeping tent is 16 x 30 feet and holds six cots. Luxuries include cement floors, electricity and mosquito netting over our beds. Potable water is delivered in five-gallon cans daily.*

*Nearby a long row of house trailers with constantly humming AC wall units reminds me of the special treatment given Air Force officers. In spite of this unfairness, the ingenuity of the American soldier is evidenced everywhere. In front of these olive-drab tents that we call home are signs reading, "God's Little Acre," "Peyton Place," and "Hotel Utah." Palm trees, banana trees, and other greenery are planted around the tents.*

*The heat is intense as it radiates from acres of white sand. It comes over my shoe tops whenever I step off the cement slab to walk anywhere in our camp, but on the bright side, slogging in sand is good exercise for my leg muscles.*

*Nearby is a white, powdery beach. As I walked in the calm, crystal clear water, fish in a multitude of colors swam around my feet. Stunning. Unlike the North Carolina coast, the mountains here are only a few hundred yards from the beach. Someday this area will probably be a tourist destination.*

*The Army Officers' Club and mess, as well as the enlisted men's club, is composed of a series of tents. In the officers' mess, Vietnamese waitresses wear native clothing—the ao dai—white, blue or black silk pants with a long-sleeved, mandarin-collared sheer dress, which comes to the ankles. Buttons extend from the collar to the waist, where it splits at the sides forming two flaps. Stunning, modest and sexy.*

*There are about 30,000 native Vietnamese in the villages surrounding Cam Ranh Bay. The people appear extremely poor and depend almost entirely on the Americans for employment. The women, who wear typical peasant clothing of black cotton pants and long-sleeved shirt, wander from tent to tent asking to wash our clothes or clean our tent.*

*The sweltering heat during the day usually reaches 100 degrees, but it cools off at night for sleeping. The difference in hot weather here and back home is that here there is no cool place to escape it. The monsoons won't begin until October, so it is also dry. I'm constantly eating dirt and sand.*

*Our medical dispensary will be moving in four days to Phan Rang, which is 30 miles south, to set up permanently. I am ready to move out of this temporary camp and set up my clinic .*

I vividly remember Cam Ranh Bay. Hot, white sand was everywhere, leading to the deep-water bay on an inlet of the South China Sea and situated on the southeastern coast of Vietnam, between Nha Trang to the north and Phan Rang to the south. Saigon (now Ho Chi

Minh City) is approximately 180 miles southwest.

The U.S. Army, Air Force and Navy built a vast supply complex and airfields over 100 square miles of sand. The Air Force operated a large cargo facility, which became the Cam Ranh Air Base used as a tactical fighter base, as well as for troop transportation. The Navy operated a major port facility, including exclusive contracts with RMK-BRJ (Raymond International, Morrison-Knudsen, Brown & Root, and J.A. Jones Construction), which built bridges, roads, ports, and airfields in South Vietnam. Calling itself "the Vietnam Builders" the contractors received highly lucrative no-bid contracts. From 1964-1972, the U.S. spent over $5 billion per month (adjusted for inflation) in Vietnam.

Cam Ranh Bay typified the military-industrial complex that President Eisenhower warned of in his 1961 farewell address. He cautioned our country against military policies and the power of the industries that profit from war materials.

Sadly, pockets are lined through lucrative arms deals as the military-industrial complex continues in wars in Afghanistan, Iran, and throughout the Middle East. In 2003, within weeks of ending combat in Iraq the federal government began handing out sweet deals to American corporations to rebuild Iraq's infrastructure. And, just as in Vietnam, those with the closest relationships to government officials were on the inside track with greater access to the enormous sums of money pouring into Iraq. The non-partisan Congressional Research Service estimated the cost of Bush and Cheney's Iraq War at over $800 billion. After adding the cost of long-term medical care and disability for veterans, estimates of the cost have ranged from 1.7 to 6 trillion dollars—and the monetary value pays no heed to the massive impact that war wages on human lives.

President Eisenhower also addressed the nation's defense budget and the on-going armaments race with the Soviet Union: "Every gun that is made, every warship launched, every rocket fired signifies, in the final sense, is a theft from those who hunger and are not fed, those who are cold and are not clothed."

President Johnson did not heed his predecessor's warnings as he began the military buildup in Vietnam. Johnson stated that the U.S. could have both guns (defense/military) and butter (domestic goods/services). The financial cost of the war destroyed his domestic War on Poverty and rewarded the defense contractors.

For me, the seed of cynicism of government and war was planted in Cam Ranh Bay. I saw more evidence of the gigantic military buildup later when I visited Tan Son Nhut Airbase complex outside Saigon. My cynicism has grown over the years as our government continues to fund wars in the Middle East for the profit of military contractors at the expense of taxpayers. Where are the legislators that will speak up to stop this madness?

# ON THE ROAD TO PHAN RANG

***4 August 1966***

*The Air Force terminal at Cam Ranh is quite plush in comparison to the surrounding military buildings. The huge Quonset hut is furnished with cushioned chairs and sofas, and the partitioned areas are maple wood paneling. An English-speaking Vietnamese woman greeted us at the check-in counter.*

*This morning I had my first aerial view of Vietnam. Capt. Youkilis, Lt. Walker, Sgt. Hill and I flew from Cam Ranh Bay to Phan Rang for a medical planning mission. There were 40 other passengers and baggage aboard the 123 Provider. (The Fairchild C-123 Provider is an American military transport aircraft built for the United States Air Force and used widely in Southeast Asia.)*

*The flight was almost as bad as flying Piedmont Airlines*, minus the stewardess.*

*The seats were made of orange canvas webbing, which folded down from the cabin wall. I took my military fatigue cap off and wiped the sweat from my forehead; it was boiling hot inside this C-123 fat*

* In North Carolina, the only airline choice I remember was Piedmont or Eastern Airlines. Piedmont merged into today's American Airline, which also obtained many of Eastern's routes.

*bird. The noise from the twin-propeller engines almost drowned out the Air Force sergeant as he gave us warning signals for fire and emergency landing (crashing). I felt uneasy about this flight, which reminded me of some old John Wayne war movie that I had never seen—and I was part of the action.*

*Actual airtime was only 12 minutes. By jeep or truck it takes over an hour to travel the 30 miles due to the poor road conditions. During this brief flight we passed over mountains, ocean, coconut groves, banana groves and rice paddies. And I thought: What a waste to destroy this beautiful countryside with war. What is to be gained?*

*Power. Money.*

*Arriving at Phan Rang Airport, I watched five F-100s take off in quick succession. I was told I could accompany a pilot on an F 100 mission. Don't think so.*

*The terminal is very small—the size of a bus station in a small U.S. town—and has no hint of the plushness of Cam Ranh Airport. A sign painted crudely on one small building outside the airport read: "Number 10 Go-Go Club." In the Vietnamese/English slang, number one is good; number 10 is very bad. This number code can be applied to anything: food, facilities, injuries, women...you name it. There is no grade in between. A number 10 club indicates a definite loser.*

*The Air Force complex was huge and consisted of wooden tropical buildings, Quonset huts and supply dumps built on a sere landscape. We traveled the short distance from the Phan Rang air terminal to the dispensary by jeep. The dispensary consisted of three Quonset huts, staffed by one medical doctor, one dentist, several enlisted medical corpsmen and eight Vietnamese workers.*

*The engineers had apparently bulldozed the area before erecting the Quonset huts and tents for the dispensary and base camp for the 101st Airborne, 1st Brigade. There was not a plant or tree in sight, and dust soon covered my uniform and sweaty face. Late afternoon our plane left Phan Rang on the same 123 Provider headed back to Cam Ranh Bay. I was tired and dirty but looking forward to the move.*

### *6 August*

*I took the opportunity to escape from Cam Ranh Bay ahead of the remainder of our company. Our entire dispensary—including men, equipment, and medicine—is to move later this week. The medical dispensary in Phan Rang requested an officer to sign for the equipment transfer. I volunteered.*

*Lt. Tucker and his jeep driver picked me up around 1730; we would need to get to Phan Rang before dark. Although it is only a 30-mile trip, the dusty road is mostly one lane, narrow, full of potholes, with rickety wooden bridges (or sometimes no bridge at all) over small streams feeding into rice paddies. Highway 1 is the main road stretching over 1,000 miles from Hanoi to Saigon and is not a highway by U.S. standards, but more like a rural road.*

*The brush along the side of the road is perfect cover for an ambush attack by Charlie. The name Charlie is a term derived from the phonetic alphabet words used by the military in radio or telephone messages to avoid confusion between similar-sounding letters. Thus "Victor Charlie," VC, is the name given to the Viet Cong guerrilla soldiers.*

*Vietnamese heavily travel the road, and we were the only jeep traveling without the protection of a convoy of military vehicles. It was rush hour on Highway 1—or based on the bad condition of the road, I would call it Highway Number 10. All the workers were walking home or using transportation of every conceivable means: motorbikes, bicycles, motorcycles, three-wheeled French cars, buses, trucks and ox carts. Old women balanced bananas in baskets hanging from poles on their shoulders. And everyone "aimed" his vehicle to the middle of the road.*

*Our driver beeped his horn and in the nick of time pedestrians and drivers got out of our way. Most drivers were traveling much too fast for the poor road conditions and swerved from side to side to avoid the biggest potholes. We kept a steady speed of 30–40 mph. I don't know how we avoided killing someone with our jeep.*

*The scenery varied from beauty to desolation. For some time we drove near the ocean, which was uninhabited, clean, and refreshing. Palm trees appeared scattered haphazardly in the landscape. Later we passed cactus and small shrubs on flat, dusty red land. To the west were blue-green mountains. A few miles further we came upon acres and acres of lush, green rice paddies. In the deeper trenches of the paddies, families were taking their baths. One man washed his feet and then urinated in the same spot. (It seems that sequence was in the right order.)*

*I have been on Maxwell Street, Chicago's skid row, and driven though the outskirts of Monterey, Mexico, but nothing I have seen compares to the abject poverty, filth, and stench I experience, while driving past primitive hamlets and villages. The dwellings range from run-down houses with a French colonial facade to small huts with thatched roofs. Surrounding the huts were wooden fences, which enclosed cattle and chickens. Naked children ran around in the same muddy, grassless yards. Small isolated huts also appear in desolate areas. In front of one of these huts I saw four boys enjoying a cockfight.*

*In every hamlet and along the highway children wave or salute, calling "Hi" or "Hello." Twenty years ago I imagine the children of another generation waved when the French passed through. Maybe they also wave when Charlie passes through their village. What can they do but smile, wave, and hope?*

*We passed through one area called "the strip," according to our driver. The village is composed entirely of bars and houses of prostitution. The fronts of the buildings are painted in bright colors with signs: "Hotel Pleasure," "Las Vegas Club," "New Yorker," etc.*

*I have heard that next to selling rice, prostitution seems to be the biggest business in this part of the country. The American military top brass permitted the strip project to be built and enforced the rule: all girls must be checked periodically by a medic and issued an I.D. card. If a soldier or airman contracts a venereal disease, he goes to the strip and points out the girl, and she will get a shot of penicillin. Any girl caught working without a card is thrown out.*

*Everything was going fine; the girls and local proprietors were making money, the morale of the troops was high, and the V.D. rate was low. But Brigadier General Pearson is up for another star and doesn't want to take chances with unfavorable publicity.* Time *magazine recently printed an article about a military-sanctioned prostitute strip in another area of Vietnam, so Pearson closed down all the strips. Now the girls and proprietors are out of work, the morale of the troops is down, and the V.D. rate is up.*

*By dusk, our jeep was the only vehicle on the road. We passed through a quiet stretch in the road and approached a coconut grove. Overhead the coconut palms formed a verdant canopy nearly blocking out the fading sky. Charlie could be hiding behind the camouflage provided by the palm trees. As a precaution, Lt. Tucker picked up his M14 rifle from the floorboard and held it ready to fire. I gripped my .45 pistol.*

*Up ahead we saw a large crowd of Vietnamese peasants. As we drove closer it was clear what the people had gathered to witness: an Army fuel truck had overturned on the side of the road into a rice paddy. The driver—still inside the cabin—lay dead, submerged in a foot of water. A fire truck and the military police had arrived.*

*There was nothing we could do. I cannot rationalize the death of another American soldier in this steaming, tropical, desolate country.*

# NHA TRANG

***10 August 1966***

*Today at 1530 hours Lt. Walker drove me in the jeep from the dispensary to the Phan Rang airport. While waiting for the plane to leave for Nha Trang, I noticed a handsome young Vietnamese man. He had long, black, shiny hair, which he combed meticulously while looking in a pocket mirror. He probably weighs about 110 pounds and stands 5'2—a typical-looking lean-bodied Vietnamese man. He walked across the terminal introducing himself as Binh Nguyen and sat down beside me.*

*"Are you a cadet officer?" he asked. (I don't know why he asked me this question. Perhaps it is because I look younger than my age.) That led to the next question.*

*"How old are you?"*

*"I'm 24," I said.*

*"Me also."*

*According to Binh, as the oldest in a family of seven children, he supports his elderly parents. He is an interpreter for the military, having learned English from a Vietnamese teacher in high school. Someday, after the war, he plans to return to Da Lat to continue his studies majoring in English.*

*As I left the terminal building to board my plane he shook my hand and asked, "Can I visit you at your home?"*

*"Sure. I will see you when I return from Nha Trang."*

As I reread this account in my journal, I realized that Binh was probably hitting on me. He must have had "gaydar" to sense that I was gay even when I didn't admit it to myself. In retrospect, I think I was oblivious to what was going on— or perhaps I was intrigued, but afraid of the possible consequences. I didn't follow up.

***10 August (continued)***

*My delayed flight arrived at 1830—after duty hours—and I didn't know who to call for transportation and lodging. No one was sitting at the military transportation desk, and the bus service is very unreliable. I hitched a ride on a truck with two other officers and together we went to numerous hotels searching for lodging. After two hours we all found lodging. It was raining, and I arrived soaking wet to a villa that housed medical officers of the 8th Field Hospital. It was so sweet to have a real twin bed, running hot and cold water, and a flushing toilet!*

*The next morning I shaved with steaming water and set out to tour the 8th Field Hospital complex. The hospital, which began in tents, is now housed in stucco and wooden buildings joined together with open-air, roofed walkways. The hospital is spread out over a wide area with many of the buildings completely air-conditioned. A Vietnamese woman—dressed in black silk pants and matching long-sleeved shirt and conical straw hat—is meticulously raking and smoothing the sand around the buildings. Flowers are blooming in the sand next to the walkways.*

*My official business here was to meet with the optical lab officer to establish procedures for sending optical prescriptions and determine the lab's capabilities. That objective was quickly accomplished, but I wanted to see the town. An optometrist friend, Herb Davis from Savannah, is visiting Nha Trang substituting for the optometrist who is away on leave. Herb managed to find a truck and gave me a tour.*

*A street near the beach was recently built by the Vietnamese with American money, expertise, equipment and materials. I was told that this was a good example of what the Vietnamese could do with American money.*

*In the evening Herb and I went shopping. One shop sold ivory and teak woodcarvings—very expensive. I bought a fatigue cap from Ambassador's Tailors, whose proprietor appeared to be Indian. The shop has pictures of Bob Hope looking at merchandise during one of his Vietnam Christmas show tours.*

***12 August***

*I walked the few blocks from the villa where I am staying down to the beach to soak in the sun and surf. Soon sand was covering most of my body as I tried to position myself on a small bath towel. Spotting an American who obviously needed a straw mat, a teenaged barefoot Vietnamese boy approached me. He wanted to sell me a straw mat for 350 piasters (Ps)—about $3.50, or three times the hourly minimum wage in the USA. I offered to pay 150 Ps.*

*"For 150 Ps you only get mat this size," he said as he showed me a mat which was less than half the size of the large mat. "275," he pleaded as I shook my head indicating no. "It number one mat...250...225..." He began to roll up the mat. Just as I thought he was going to leave because my price had insulted him, he said, "O.K. you can have for 200."*

*Although the mat was overpriced, I felt it was worth 200 Ps for his dramatic, enthusiastic presentation. He had his bartering technique down to an art. As he got up from the sand, he said, "I leave you now." I watched as he walked down the beach to make as many Ps as possible from another American soldier.*

*I returned to the hospital complex around 1400 hours and caught a ride with an ambulance driver to return to Phan Rang. As we drove through the familiar coconut grove, a medic riding with us fired off a magazine of ammunition. We didn't see Viet Cong; he was wasting ammunition to theoretically harass the invisible guerrilla soldiers. It had been a long, hot, dirty, and potentially dangerous trip, but we made it safely without an incident.*

*And I had a new straw mat.*

I don't remember being afraid while we were traveling through the coconut grove. Perhaps, like many young men, I felt invincible. Visiting Nha Trang was a new adventure—from meeting Binh in the airport to my day on the South China Sea beach.

Nha Trang was a small town then, but today it has grown to a city of 400,000 located on the beautiful Nha Trang Bay and is a popular tourist destination. Nha Trang is surrounded on all three sides by mountains and a large island on the fourth side.

At the time I was in Nha Trang, I didn't know that within a year I would travel to two other beautiful bays in the world—in Hong Kong, where I would date a woman, and in Rio de Janeiro, where I would date a man.

# CITIZENSHIP

***11 August 1966***

*Today I talked at great length with Joe, a young man who was born in West Germany and is now serving with the 101st Airborne. He was confused, disillusioned, and disappointed. Joe lived with his family in Communist East Germany until 1960, when his family defected to West Berlin. He was one of over three million people who left for a better life in the West before the Berlin Wall was completed. At seventeen he left West Germany to study at the University of Wisconsin.*

*He quit the university and joined the army. After completing basic training, he took a test to enter Officer Candidate School and passed all requirements except one. He was not an American citizen. He then applied for a warrant officer commission with special interest in flying helicopters. He met the first requirement, which was that he is at least eighteen, but failed requirement two—he was not an American citizen. Citizenship is required for a security clearance.*

*But Joe wouldn't give up. He applied for Special Forces training but again didn't qualify because he was not a citizen. As a last resort for advanced achievement he applied for airborne training. He made it and proudly wears his airborne wings.*

*Last year he was sent along with over forty thousand U.S. troops to the Dominican Republic to end fighting and install a non-military government. (President Lyndon Johnson feared the unrest would result in a communist dictatorship like Cuba.),*

*Now for the irony. Joe has been wounded twice and is fighting for a country of which he is not a citizen. His main concern was facing society after leaving the army in seven months. His English vocabulary has shrunk to a basic fifty words—mostly curse words. His family is concerned about his well-being. He is only twenty-one, and he realizes that he has been in the army during his formative years. His only escape from his environment has been to drink himself into oblivion. The good news is that in seven months he will be discharged and will receive his U.S. citizenship.*

*Good luck, Joe.*

My conversation with Joe was the first time I had considered immigration issues. He was fortunate to qualify under special provisions of the Immigration and Nationality Act, which expedites the application and naturalization process for members of the U.S. armed forces, who must demonstrate good moral character, knowledge of the English language, and the U.S. government. In the past fifteen years, U.S. Citizen and Immigration Services has naturalized 89,095 members of the military, 1,898 of their spouses, and 76 of their children in ceremonies in 28 countries.

While naturalization is viewed as a liberal issue in today's political culture, it was actually President Reagan who legalized undocumented immigrants through the bipartisan Immigration Reform and Control Act of 1986. The bill awarded green cards to 2.7 million people with a clear path to citizenship, but it left behind over 2 million people unauthorized because they arrived in the U.S. after 1982. In addition, Congress didn't allocate enough funding for effective border control. Illegal immigration continued.

Four years later, another Republican President, George H.W. Bush, and a Democratic controlled Congress, signed the next immigration bill, which introduced a visa lottery for residents of specific countries and increased the number of nonimmigrant visas for highly skilled workers. Significant to me in this new law was elimination of restrictions that prevented immigrants from entering because of their homosexuality and against immigrants who were HIV-positive.

Illegal immigration continued, and in June 2013 the U.S. Senate voted 68-32 for a bipartisan bill to overhaul immigration laws creating a path to citizenship for millions of undocumented residents, while ratcheting up security along the Mexican border. The Republican House of Representatives refused to pass the Senate's immigration bill. The Obama administration tried unsuccessfully to pass the "Dream Act," which would stop deporting children who met certain conditions. Circumventing immigration law, Obama directed the Secretary of Homeland Security to stop deporting people younger than thirty who came to the United States before the age of sixteen, pose no criminal or security threat, and are successful students or served in the military. These people can get a two-year deferral from deportation.

What will happen to these registered immigrants in the future? What will happen to U.S.-born children of immigrants when their parents are deported? If we believe the Republican rhetoric, the future of immigrants is not bright. Today, as immigration reform stalls in a hyper-partisan congress, it is imperative that we develop a clear, concise, and just path to citizenship.

We are all immigrants or descendants of immigrants, unless we are Native Americans. In my family, both the Whiteners and the Reeps are descendants of German immigrants. They came to this country before 1875, when the U.S. began restricting immigration. Without their immigration I would not be where I am or who I am today.

President Trump ran on an anti-immigration platform. After his election, my friend Abdul realized that his son would not be safe in America. Born in Trinidad to Indian and Muslim parents, his family arranged a marriage for him, which produced a son. As a closeted gay man, Abdul was forced to choose between living a life of secrecy or escaping his traditionalist background. The marriage ended with him and his son fleeing to the U.S. as undocumented immigrants. One month after the election of Trump, he sent his 16-year-old son to live with his aunt in Canada—a safe haven for immigrants and refugees. Abdul, fearing each day that he will be deported, still works in the United States.

Also, my thoughts on citizenship turn to gentle, soft-spoken Josefa. In the 1940s, she and her husband immigrated to Southern California, where they worked as farmers. Tony (my future husband) and I had been together for many years when we began visiting Josefa, who was his grandmother. She sensed our love and commitment and always made me feel welcome. On one of our annual visits to El Centro, she proudly showed Tony and me her U.S. citizenship paper, which she received at age eighty-two—nearly sixty years after arriving in the United States.

At the end of each visit, she took my hands and placed them on top of Tony's hands, wrapping her hands around ours, and gave us a blessing, which I interpreted as invoking God's favor and giving us her approval. She was not a rich woman, and the blessing was all she had to give. At the end of each visit, she told us she wouldn't live until the next trip; yet, she continued the annual ritual until her death over ten years later.

Immigration has a face: people like Joe, like Abdul, like Josefa, and all of the people working and fighting for a nation that denies them citizenship.

# ONLY IN AMERICA

***15 August 1966***

*Jim Mahoney and I were relaxing in the air-conditioned 101st Airborne's Quonset hut library. I was peacefully reading Harry Golden's book,* Only in America, *and enjoying his liberal Jewish satire about life in the South.*

*Without warning a soldier opened the door and said, "Have you heard about the red light alert?"*

*Stupid question. If we had known about an alert, would we be sitting there? "Assume your alert station," the soldier said.*

*He was serious.*

*Jim ran to our jeep to "assume our alert station." I grudgingly dropped my book, and left the quiet sanctuary of the library.*

*"What's the security password for the day?" Jim asked as he turned on the jeep's ignition.*

*"I don't know. Yesterday it was 'peach something.'"*

*"Thanks a lot," he sarcastically muttered.*

*Although I was calm compared to Jim, I was concerned, because at supper the previous evening Capt. Brown mentioned that there had been enemy action at the water supply point, not far from our camp.*

*Jim headed the jeep toward our dispensary, speeding more*

*than usual. As our jeep came to a screeching halt in front of the dispensary, we noticed everyone was armed with either rifles or pistols and wearing helmets and battle gear. Our weapons and ammunition were locked up in a metal cargo container—for safekeeping and to prevent us from accidentally shooting each other or ourselves.*

*Lt. Walker calmly informed us that there was some action "somewhere" and thus the alert status.*

*Alert or no alert, I had to use the latrine. The alert was called off by the time I had finished my business.*

*We returned to the library, and I resumed reading Harry Golden's satire.*

The 101st library was an air-conditioned sanctuary. With few distractions I had free time to read for the first time in my life. Because of the limited number of choices, I read authors, whose work normally I would not have chosen: Ayn Rand, Friedrich Nietzsche, C.S. Lewis, George Orwell, and Harry Golden.

For over twenty-five years Harry Golden was a reporter for the North Carolina-based *Labor Journal* and *The Charlotte Observer*. He wrote in a satirical style about politics and the absurdities of life, including racial segregation and the state's Jim Crow laws. His "Vertical Negro Plan" proposed removing the stools or chairs from any soon-to-be-integrated buildings, since Southern whites didn't mind standing with blacks, only sitting with them.

As a Jew, a Southern minority, Golden wrote from a unique viewpoint, and I appreciated his use of humor to break down prejudice. Golden didn't correlate racial discrimination with homosexual discrimination, but if he were alive today, I hope he would be writing about inequality and discrimination affecting gays and lesbians, just as he powerfully advocated for racial equality in the 1950s.

# SUNDAY IN THE SQUARE WITH GENE

***21 August 1966***

*The camp was unusually quiet because most men in our unit were sleeping late. After breakfast I drove alone to the 101st Chapel, which was located in a large tent with 50-60 metal folding chairs.*

*It was standing-room only today, and I soon discovered the reason. The majority of the attendees were men who worked at the civilian construction company, which gives a half-day off if they attend church—otherwise they had to work.*

*The scripture was from Isaiah: "For thou hast been a strength to the needy in his distress, a refuge from the storm, a shadow from the heat..." We sang three hymns and recited the Lord's Prayer. I understand that it is difficult to meet the spiritual needs of men from varied Protestant backgrounds, but the chaplain delivered another lackluster homily.*

*In the afternoon Gene Fishman and I drove to Phan Rang, about five miles away. In the village square a crowd was gathered to watch two monkeys perform under a palm tree. Across the square was a new Volkswagen bus equipped with a loudspeaker that was hawking medicines. A woman was feeding sugarcane into a machine and producing thick syrup.*

*On a side street was a barbershop where male barbers provided not only haircuts and shaves, but also sexual favors (or so I was told). I never checked it out.*

*I watched a young dentist, who wore a polo shirt and aviator sunglasses. His market space (located next to a merchant selling tin cans) consisted of a table displaying pulled teeth and a sign that indicated his hours were 8 to 12. He injected a needle into the gum of a child, no more than seven years old. Sitting next to the boy was his younger brother and an anxious-looking mother. After the anesthesia took effect, he pulled the tooth. To my amazement, the boy didn't make a sound.*

*The children I saw in the village do not appear to be malnourished. As they approached us with outstretched dirty hands begging for money, I remember a similar scene from visiting Monterey, Mexico. Several of the children felt my pockets for money. Their English vocabulary consists of "Sorry about that," "No sweat, G.I.," "Hello," and a few curse words. I found it difficult to refuse these dirty, naked, innocent-looking little kids, but if I gave money to one, I would be mobbed. A small boy—perhaps five years old and wearing only a shirt—followed us around the market for about 45 minutes.*

*Most everything is displayed on tables in the market—clothing, hardware, pottery, jewelry, Army C rations, beer, charcoal, freshly cut flowers and straw mats. Fresh tropical fruit and local vegetables are sold next to vendors of fish, meat and live ducks. I attributed the market's farrago of scents to urine and fish.*

*I bought a ceramic teapot with a painted oriental design, a straw mat, and a chain to secure our steering wheel on the jeep for a total of 350 Ps, or four American dollars. Good deal.*

*Near the market was a palm-tree-lined residential area with iron-gated, French colonial houses. There is a cinema and many bars—including the infamous "Miami Bar," where you can buy booze and the company of women.*

*A short walk from the market we discovered a street with pedicabs, bicycles and, unexpectedly, an Esso service station. The irony was seeing a service station when we had seen only two vehicles in town. And "service station" must have a different meaning here, because I saw an old lady—her lips and teeth stained red from chewing betel nut—squatting at the curb next to the Esso station. With her shirttail strategically covering her private parts she somehow pulled down her black pajamas just far enough to urinate. I was on sensory overload. It was time to leave.*

*With no TV or other diversions this evening (and most other evenings), Gene, Ron and I sat in front of our tents to be entertained and awed by the sunset-spectacular: streaks of yellow-gold, orange-tangerine and flaming ochre, interspersed with steely gray clouds against a sky colored cobalt blue to purple, outlining the darkening distant hills. The climax of a good day.*

From my earliest memory, I began every Sunday by attending church. This Sunday in Vietnam was no different. The Hebrew scripture reading promised me that God was my strength and shelter in the time of storm. In future days I would need that reassurance.

As I look again at the Kodachrome photos I took, the images of the busy marketplace come to life. There is a sense of order and beauty in the photo of 15 hand-woven shallow baskets filled with red and green chili peppers and an equal number of local women with their straw conical hats. Time improves the appreciation for that marketplace and the village.

If I were to return to Vietnam, I would see a scene similar to that day in 1967: women in the central market selling chili peppers, fresh vegetables, fish, clothing and services useful to the locals. I am pleased to know that this tradition hasn't changed.

# DRINKING IN DA LAT

***5 September 1966***

*The rough road from Phan Rang to Da Lat (only 30 miles northwest of Phan Rang) passes through tropical vegetation and a tea plantation, which serve as potential VC ambush cover. But I went by plane to visit Capt. George Schnetzer, who came over on the ship with me.*

*At an altitude of 5,000 feet, Da Lat is a beautiful mountain resort town. The occupying French built villas here to escape the heat and humidity of Saigon. With its year-round temperate weather, farmers grow tomatoes, lettuce, cabbage, cucumbers, carrots, onions, and radishes for salads served to GIs—and the Viet Cong guerrillas.*

*Although most of the French have left, their architecture remains. The big villas are surrounded by extensive gardens flourishing with poinsettia bushes as high as seven feet, hydrangea and roses. The smell of thousands of pine trees, the cool air and the lakes all reminded me of home—and helped restore a small measure of serenity in me. For all the serenity of a mountain resort town, it also offers entertainment at numerous bars, restaurants and clubs, which serve American GIs. The most notorious cathouse is the G.P.—Green Pisser—named so by GIs in spite of the fact that the bar doesn't have a latrine. (Green piss is GI slang for gonorrhea.)*

*Driving by the small house, I could see action on the screened front porch. (By all means, let's keep out mosquitoes to prevent malaria; never mind the other diseases transmitted inside the G.P.) I was told that from the 350 U.S. troops stationed here, 33 cases of VD were recorded last month and most can be traced back to the G.P. establishment. I suppose the tension of war is relieved in many ways.*

*Another hot spot in town is the "Tulip Rouge," a restaurant and bar owned by Mr. Rosenburger, who is from Switzerland. Mrs. Rosenburger, a French woman, serves up Vietnamese/French food in the Tulip. George said it is a nice place and is frequented by Nguyen Cao Ky, President of South Vietnam, and other dignitaries.*

*I am staying in a villa owned by Major General Tree of the Republic of Vietnam (RVN) forces. He is breaking his lease with the U.S. military in order to raise the rent from $400 a month—an amount equal to one month of military pay for me. General Tree is leaving the country soon for Washington as part of General Westmoreland's staff.*

*If it weren't in a country at war, Da Lat would be nearly perfect. The temperature seldom reaches higher than the 70s in the day and in the 50s at night. Both the bedroom and living rooms in our villa have fireplaces, and at night a fire in the fireplace is welcomed.*

*There are several important institutions in town including the National Military Academy (similar to our West Point), a nuclear research center, Da Nhin hydroelectric project, and the Pasteur Institute, which manufactures most of the vaccines for South Vietnam. There are a number of boarding schools, as well as the University Institute of Da Lat which is spread out on the hills north of Xuan Huong Lake.*

*Capt. George Schnetzer is the primary care physician for the troops stationed here. He is certain there will be hostile action before the September 11th election and believes the Viet Cong will blow up a villa or hotel downtown. According to George, there was a villa blown up last December. No one knows if the perpetrator was VC or a disgruntled construction worker who had been fired.*

*The same week Schnetzer arrived at the clinic there was an attempt to destroy his ambulance—his only means of transportation. By mistake the gas tank was filled with diesel fuel. After driving several miles the ambulance began smoking and then stopped. The driver discovered what had occurred and began draining the fuel tank.*

*A crowd of Vietnamese formed around the vehicle. A few minutes later the driver looked up and saw a trail of fire proceeding toward the ambulance. Someone had dropped a match to the stream of diesel fuel and fled. Fortunately, a military wrecker was passing by and saw what was happening. He immediately pushed the ambulance away from the burning fuel. If there had been a large amount of gasoline mixed in the diesel fuel, the result would have been disastrous.*

*Tension between the Vietnamese and American soldiers is running high. Any GI who remotely resembles a troublemaker is immediately kicked out of town. One military policeman was dating a local Vietnamese singer—Miss RVN Air Force of 1965—who happened to be married to a RVN Air Force officer. The woman's husband warned the MP to cease play, but he persisted. The husband then publicly announced he would kill the soldier. The officer had "lost face" in society and had to avenge his enemy. The military immediately flew the MP out of town. I don't know the outcome of the situation, but rumor has it that there were Vietnamese Air Force men who met his plane when it landed.*

*Danger can be anywhere. One never knows for certain who is Charlie—until he strikes. He can be a guard, a boy on a bicycle riding on the street, a construction worker or an innocent-looking vegetable seller in the marketplace.*

*Unlike battlefields in World War II, there are no front lines in guerrilla warfare. There is a 24-hour guard detail at most villas. The dispensary is guarded at night by its own corpsmen. There are Vietnamese guards at some villas, but if faced with danger they would probably be the first to flee. Our villa is unguarded, so we sleep at night with loaded pistols on the table beside our beds.*

*Tonight I was invited to a party. When I arrived at Villa 19 at 1730, the party, which had begun two hours earlier, was well underway. I followed the sound of music—the Rolling Stones' "I Can't Get No Satisfaction"—and entered Maj. Jackson's apartment. I was startled to see an American woman dancing around the bedroom. There are few American women in Vietnam. Old Kay (everyone referred to each other as old so-and-so) was in her late 20s, tall and thin with straight, dark brown hair, which touched the collar of her white blouse. She wore a pale blue short skirt. Surrounding her and swaying to the music were seven officers: Col. Walker, Col. Jones, Maj. Jackson, Maj. Miller, Capt. Schnetzer, Capt. Smith and Mr. McDonald (warrant officer). It was not yet obvious who was Kay's date for the evening.*

*Maj. Miller appeared the drunkest of the lot. Slurring his words he informed me, "I am going to hell."*

*"I'll drink to that," said Capt. Smith.*

*"I know I am," repeated Maj. Miller.*

*"Now, you don't know that," said Mr. McDonald.*

*"I wish I had three fine sons like you, Jim," Maj. Jackson turned back to speak to Mr. McDonald.*

*"They're just like any other boys. They get into quite a few situations."*

*"If I only had a son," repeated Maj. Jackson. "Yes, I know I'm going to hell. I've talked with the Lord several times about it. You see what war does to a person, Lieutenant? You live while you can. You squeeze all the life out of every moment of time because it may be our last. You ought to be ready to go anytime. Make sure you're a Christian. That's the important thing."*

*"I'll drink to that," Col. Jones shouted.*

*"How old are you, Lieutenant?" Mr. McDonald asked me.*

*"Twenty-four."*

*"I was in the Army six months when you were born. It's been a long time," sighed Mr. McDonald.*

*"I have been in three wars." Col. Walker held up three fingers.*

*"Three wars? I don't think I'm that old." Laughter. "Let's drink to the wars, starting with the Civil War," proposed Col. Jones.*

*"I missed that one," said Capt. Smith.*

*All: "I'll drink to that."*

*"How about the Spanish-American War?"*

*"I'll drink to that."*

*"War number one."*

*"I missed that one."*

*"War number two."*

*"I remember that one."*

*"How could you forget it? That was a real war."*

*"I'll drink to that."*

*"Korean conflict. That was a cold mother."*

*"And this one—what do they call this one?"*

*Maj. Jackson turned to me. "You've been observing this party long enough. I don't like spectators. You're going to drink some of my whiskey." He shoved a half-filled glass of whiskey into my hands.*

*"But--"*

*"No buts. Don't put that glass down."*

*The Major was obviously drunk. I didn't know what to do. I had never been ordered to drink by a superior officer and knew it was an insult to refuse to drink his whiskey. I falteringly tried to explain that every man had to decide for himself what was right and wrong. I remember mumbling something about having "to live with myself." This must have struck a chord. I think that he might have had a difficult time living with himself. He was separated from his wife and was probably having an affair with Kay—a young woman half his age. He dropped the order for me to drink.*

*Captains Wright and Schnetzer, Mr. McDonald, and I left for supper. When we returned an hour later the taped music playing was the Supremes' "You Keep Me Hangin' On." Everyone—including Old Kay—was still partying. Old Janice, an American schoolteacher about 21 years old and employed by USAID for two years of duty in Vietnam, had joined the party. She appeared considerably reserved and was not playing the flirting game, unlike her roommate, Old Kay. I couldn't handle the drinking scene and returned to Capt. Schnetzer's villa around 2100.*

*Around 0200, a banging on the door awakened us. It was the*

*Major begging for his jeep key to take Old Kay home. (It seems that Old Kay is the Major's girlfriend, after all.)*

*Earlier in the evening Schnetzer had taken the jeep key from Maj. Jackson for his own safety. According to Schnetzer, who looks after the Old Major as if he were his elderly father, every time the Major gets drunk, which is quite often, he loads up his jeep with ammunition, and drives through the village and surrounding area firing his weapon. He is certain that the Old Major will be shot one night during these escapades.*

*"Come on, pal...you're a good buddy...you old rat's ass," babbled the Major.*

*"Have you sobered up?" asked Schnetzer.*

*"Yes, and I've got to take Kay home."*

*"I don't want you driving through the village and acting foolish, sir."*

*Throwing in "sir" after the reprimand by Schnetzer was more than I could take at this hour. I cracked up laughing.*

*Later when we got up to go to breakfast, Schnetzer began looking for the Major's jeep key. He didn't remember admonishing the Old Major before giving him his key a few hours earlier. I did.*

***4 October 1966***

*I have returned to Da Lat. On this visit I'm staying two days in the cool, wet, blossoming paradise located in the mountains of the Central Highlands of Vietnam. The poinsettias are just as red and the pine-scented air just as fresh as I remembered.*

*Today I shopped for handcrafts made by the Montagnard people and sold in the Villa Alliance Craft Shop. I bought a Montagnard crossbow and bookmarkers with "Vietnam" woven into the fabric. The crossbow, which is similar to the bow and arrow, is touted as a quiet accurate weapon.*

*The doc I'm staying with has a French lesson tonight, so I was alone in the apartment when good old Maj. Jackson knocked on the door. I told him that I returned to Da Lat because I still didn't have my clinic equipment and thus no patients. He began a lecture about self-discipline.*

*"Use your spare time to study things that you neglected while in school. The best way to have a fruitful day," he continued, "is to make a list of things to accomplish the next day."*

*I nodded my head as the crapulent major changed the subject, "I want to show you my new speakers."*

*Jackson invited me to his nearby apartment where he proudly showed me trophies mounted on the wall—a 20-pound set of buffalo horns and a tiger skin. He had just purchased two new speakers and was in the process of hooking up the speakers to the stereo receiver. "What do you want to drink?" he asked.*

*"I don't drink alcohol, Major," I reminded him.*

*"I've had enough tonight anyway," he said. The only non-alcoholic beverage he had to offer was quinine water. So he poured me the water, said "cheers," and I gulped down the bitter-tasting liquid.*

*About 15 minutes later he said he had to pay a social call on a colonel who was in the town for the day. He invited me to come with him to a restaurant downtown and have a cup of tea with them. I had civilian clothes but only military boots, so the Major offered me his size 10EE cowboy boots. Although I wear a size 12 narrow, I somehow wiggled my feet into the short, wide boots.*

*We met the Colonel and Maj. Miller at the Shanghai Restaurant. Although I'd just eaten a big meal—including a grilled buffalo steak*—the Major ordered French onion soup and tea for us. Since both the soup and tea were boiled, I figured it was safe.*

*The Colonel was in Da Lat because of reports of numerous fights, shootings and carousing by soldiers stationed here. Maj. Jackson—AKA "Grey Ghost"—is the commanding officer, noted for his non-presence, screwing around, and a trouble-making unit. The Doc sews up soldiers from his unit practically every night. The Old Colonel promptly informed Jackson that downtown was now "off limits" for all troops until further notice.*

*Except for me and Maj. Miller—who brought his own bottle to*

---

*I describe food frequently in the diary. Being a son of the South and son of one of the best cooks ever, I appreciate good food, which continues to be a big part of the enjoyment of life.

*save money—everyone at the table continued ordering drinks (not tea). As we stood up from the table to leave, Maj. Miller handed his jeep key to the Colonel, and Miller rode back with us. The Old Colonel, whose mission in Da Lat was to shape up the troops from their notorious carousing, left the restaurant to go to the Tulip Rouge nightclub—to carouse.*

*What's the lesson here? Example is the best teacher? Or rank has its privilege?*

As I recall the two trips to Da Lat so many years ago, I am surprised at my audacity in confronting a superior officer and upholding my Christian belief in abstinence—both in sexual activity and drinking. Drinking alcohol, especially beer, was a part of military culture, and I was conspicuously in the minority who abstained.

I had no way of knowing that my faith and religious convictions about abstinence would be challenged and soon changed. My transformation from innocence (mostly) to experience came about, in part, from my travels over the next two years within Southeast Asia, and three other continents—North America, South America and Europe.

# MYH AND LINH

***10 September 1966***

*Myh and Linh are Vietnamese women who work as maids for our dispensary. Their primary work task is sweeping the floors in our dispensary and dusting. Or at least that's all I see them do. This may be their only job, since the red dust blows constantly into our tents and Quonset huts.*

*Recently, one of the medics took a photo of Myh, and after having it developed at the PX, showed her the result. Myh didn't like the photo and asked to buy it back from him. Spec. Jones said jokingly that it would cost 100 Ps. Capt. Fishman overheard the conversation and in jest added, "No, 1000 Ps."*

*The next day Myh brought Jones the 1000 Ps—which represented 11 days of her wages (about $10). He accepted the money and gave her the picture. After he had his fun, he tried to return the money, but she refused. Is this a cultural thing?*

*Linh is pregnant. She wears the typical black trousers with a long-sleeved white or black shirt. Recently she showed us a photo of herself in the beautiful, traditional ao dai with three darling children. She left her family in Da Lat to come here and earn money to support them.*

*Linh says she's in love with Spec. Falwell. She gave him a love letter that she had composed the previous night. It stated that she loved him and couldn't keep her hands off him. She even cut off her long black hair for him. Falwell is making no commitments.*

*On Tuesdays the Red Cross girl came to the holding area of our dispensary to visit the patients, who are kept here temporarily for minor ailments. When Myh saw her, she said to me, "She number one girl" and made round eyes with her hands cupped in circles over her eyes.*

As I reflect back, Myh's ponderous sign language is puzzling. Why did she think that the Red Cross girl, who was Caucasian with round eyes, made her a "number one?" Where did that come from? Why did she make herself inferior (number ten)? She had no access to TV and American movies to influence her. Perhaps her perception came from the 1950s and French women, who preceded the Red Cross women. Why did she overreact to her photo? These are conversations I wish I had.

Linh loved Falwell, but he was married and unwilling to make a commitment to her. I don't know if the father of her baby was Falwell. But I know that American soldiers fathered tens of thousands of children with Vietnamese prostitutes, girlfriends, PX workers, secretaries and maids. Fifteen years after the U.S. withdrew forces from Vietnam, Congress created the Amerasian Homecoming Act, which provided visas and resettled approximately twenty-five thousand children from U.S. troops and employees . It is disgraceful that it took so many years for Congress to recognize the problem and attempt to fix it.

There is a Vietnamese saying that reflects the condemnation of marrying outsiders: It is better to marry the village dog than a man from another village. I can only imagine the years of hardship, shunning, abuse, and shaming of the mothers and biracial children of American soldiers from "another village." Their lives became more unbearable when Saigon fell to the Communists, and these mothers were not only ostracized by society, but also vilified as "collaborators" with the American enemy. Amerasian children are another tragic example of collateral war damage.

# SAFE FOR DEMOCRACY

***11 September 1966***

*Today the election for president and members of the Constitutional Assembly is being held in South Vietnam. There have been alleged threats on the small hamlets in the surrounding area. One hamlet chief was told by the VC that all his people would be killed if they voted. In another hamlet the terrorists burned the voters' registration cards to prevent their voting. It seems about as difficult for a Vietnamese to vote here as for a Negro back home.*

Free and accessible voting is key to democracy. Although African-Americans no longer receive death threats for voting, there are other ways to discourage them from doing so. In 2013, North Carolina was added to over thirty other Republican-controlled state governments to enact a law limiting access to voting through strict photo voter ID requirements, as well as placing limitations on early voting, same-day registration and pre-registration. The law can disproportionately affect minority and older voters who may not have a government-issued photo identification card.

The law also can affect younger voters. University student IDs were deemed not acceptable for voting, and in one instance, an Appalachian State University voting site was closed. Those seventeen thousand students will need to drive off campus to a polling site with only thirty-four parking spaces.

In 2016, voters weighed in and defeated the reelection of Governor Pat McCrory. I believe his support of the voter ID law and the HB2 law legalizing discrimination against gay, lesbian and transgender people led to his defeat. Democrat Roy Cooper, who voiced opposition to both iniquitous bills, was elected.

The appellate court overturned the N.C. ID law for its discriminatory intent. Not to be deterred, Republican legislators appealed the decision. In 2017, the Supreme Court refused to hear the appeal, which keeps the law from being enforced.

Before the 1966 Vietnam election, there were a series of military-backed presidents and coups d'état until the voters elected Lieutenant General Nguyen Van Thieu president and Premier Nguyen Cao Ky vice president. In the so-called "free elections" a total of 532 candidates—22 of them women—from 3 parties ran for 117 seats in the National Assembly. No communist or pro-neutralist was permitted to run for office. Those elected were charged with drafting a new constitution to provide a basis for a new republican government. The people were promised a representative government.

The threats of decapitation, bombings, and murder by the VC terrorists did not affect the 83 percent voter turnout. Two years earlier in the U.S. presidential election only 62 percent of Americans voted. In a country that holds itself up as a model for representative democracy, low voter turnout continues to this day.

The size of the popular vote was a victory, if not for the South Vietnamese people, then at least for President Johnson's policy to promote democracy. Temporarily, this ended the U.S. embarrassment of supporting previous South Vietnam governments through three military coups in four years.

Two years earlier, Defense Secretary McNamara had visited South Vietnam and afterward advised President Johnson to increase military aid. McNamara and other policy makers were convinced that the U.S. must prevent a Communist victory in South Vietnam, believing it would damage the credibility of the U.S. globally. The war in Vietnam became a test of U.S. resolve in fighting Communism in Southeast Asia, in accordance with the "domino theory."

In 1954, President Eisenhower first referred to the domino theory in a speech about Communism in Indochina and the fear that Communism could spread from country to country:

> "Finally, you have broader considerations that might follow what you would call the 'falling domino' principle. You have a row of dominoes set up; you knock over the first one, and what will happen to the last one is the certainty that it will go over very quickly. So you could have a beginning of a disintegration that would have the most profound influences."

President Johnson was following the policy from President Eisenhower's administration, as well as President Kennedy's. The fear was that if Vietnam fell to Communism, next would be Cambodia, Laos, Thailand, and eventually all of Southeast Asia. As it turned out, the war would be Johnson's downfall.

As a person whose thirty-year career was in public health policy, I am mindful of President Johnson's other war—the War on Poverty. In 1965, he used his unique legislative skills to persuade Congress to pass Medicare, Medicaid, and Head Start. These three programs were transformational in providing health care for the elderly and low-income individuals, as well as pre-school education for children. Unfortunately, most people will remember President Johnson for his escalation of U.S. forces from a few thousand to over 500,000 troops on the ground at the height of the war. Increasing the number of troops didn't result in victory.

Sadly, we don't learn from history. Secretary of State Colin Powell, who was a soldier in Vietnam, should not have supported the invasion of Iraq. In Vietnam the U.S. faced guerrilla warfare, and in Iraq we unleashed tribal warfare—both wars were unwinnable. In addition to lives lost, both wars cost billions of dollars and left thousands of dead, wounded and disabled veterans.

Democracy is supposed to be a system of government in which people can choose representatives from competing parties through free and fair elections. In Vietnam, members of the Communist Party, who were barred from the 1966 elections, now hold 99 percent of seats in the National Assembly. It is a one-party, state-ruled, socialist country.

Woodrow Wilson said that the world must be made safe for democracy. Doing so is costly in human lives and armaments, and the outcome is never certain.

# BLESS THE BEAST AND THE CHILDREN

***20 September 1966***

*Today three enlisted men and I traveled by jeep convoy on Highway 1 to Nha Trang to pick up medical supplies. It is safer but much slower to travel via convoy, however, the two-hour journey becomes three hours. Recently there was a small battle 200 meters off the road near Nha Trang.*

*We spent the night in Nha Trang, and the next day we loaded our supplies in the jeep to return—without a convoy. According to Hanoi Hanna and America's prophetess, Jeanne Dixon*, Cam Ranh Bay is to be attacked on September 22. Since we must travel through Cam Ranh on Highway 1 on our return to our base camp, we decided not to tempt fate, and returned a day earlier than originally planned.*

*Although we avoided driving through the village and military base, the Cam Ranh Bay area is becoming a massive development as highways and other construction projects are advancing rapidly. The military is building permanent structures, which indicates that the U.S. will never leave Vietnam.*

---

*Jeanne Dixon accurately predicted President Kennedy's assassination. In 1977 I would see her eating breakfast in the Colonial Cafeteria, a Washington, D.C., landmark.

*We stopped at a small village to buy rope and Cokes, and I was left to guard our jeep and trailer. Before I knew what was happening, young kids were attempting to steal supplies from our jeep. Shouting at them had no effect. I knew something must be done quickly to restore order.*

*I pulled out my .45 caliber pistol and proceeded to point it at the kids. They immediately dropped their stolen merchandise: a can of beans and a pack of cigarettes. Although they moved away a few feet from the vehicle, I don't believe they thought I was serious. I continued to shout and wave my pistol as they stood their ground and stared at me in disbelief. The men returned to the jeep and tied down our supplies with the new rope.*

*As we continued on our way on Highway 1, the corpsmen laughed about my pistol performance. They quipped that I might qualify for the combat medic badge for my action, but I doubt that holding off child thieves merits a medal.*

Tears fill my eyes as I read this journal entry. I am far from proud about the events of that day. What possessed me to aim my pistol at children? I had heard reports that the VC recruit children to throw hand grenades at U.S. soldiers. As I impulsively pulled my pistol, perhaps I thought that the children were the enemy. After all, I was guarding the jeep, and kids were taking our supplies. But that was contrary to my military training: as a medical officer, I was to use my weapon to only protect my patients. My action remains indefensible.

The kids were attempting to steal things: a can of beans, a package of cigarettes. The kids dropped the items and ran, but what if they hadn't dropped the items? Would I have shot them? No. I am reminded of this scenario as I recently read about a police officer in Oklahoma shooting an unarmed teenager in the back of the head as he was running away from an attempted home robbery. "As he was running away," he was killed for attempting to steal something. The murder of the young boy appalls me, as does my behavior with the kids attempting to steal from my jeep.

September 20, 1966, was the first and last time I ever pointed a pistol—or any weapon—at another human being. God forgive me.

# A DAY IN THE LIFE

***3 October 1966***

*The day begins around 0630, and like other mornings the sound of clanking trashcans as soldiers are emptying the contents into a truck and tossing them back to the ground serves as my alarm clock. I struggle to wake up from the torpor of another night in the Nam, reach for my green skivvies, and eventually walk like a zombie the 100 yards to the latrine.*

*After the latrine, I manage to point myself toward the nearby Dental Clinic where I shave my sunburned face. In the beginning I used cold water for the face scraping, but now we have hot water. A pure pleasure.*

*I return to the tent where I begin the laborious routine of donning the green Army uniform—undershirt, fatigue shirt and pants, cushioned-soled socks, elastic blousing straps for the pants, and jungle boots. The black leather boots have green canvas inserts for quicker drying of the feet after soldiers wade through swamps or streams. To create a cooler short-sleeved shirt, I fold up the long sleeves to regulation length. (I roll the sleeves down at dusk to prevent mosquito bites.)*

*By now I have worked up a sweat as the morning's crispness has disappeared. I can feel the rising, tropical sun as it burns through the green canvas tent. The smell is old canvas and dust. Jim Mahoney, my tent mate, is still sleeping off another hangover from the previous night.*

*Now I am ready for a cup of coffee and a morning in the clinic. Since the equipment for my optometry clinic has not arrived—four months after I packed it for shipment at Fort Lewis—I am rather limited in a professional capacity. My empty office (other than a grey metal desk) is a plywood-partitioned 25-by-10-foot area in a Quonset hut, which I share with the laboratory and the dispensary's six beds used for transitory patients. At first it was fun having no clinical equipment and thus no work, but now I am bored. I need to find some work.*

*Within our dispensary, the sexually transmitted disease (STD) laboratory is the busiest clinic during sick call and has only one corpsman staffing it. Since the lab is understaffed, and to help occupy my time, I volunteered to draw blood and take gonorrhea smears. My hands were unsteady during the first week of on-the-job training, but I must say that I've become a capable "blood-smear" technician. Fascinating work!*

*The stories accompanying the source of the GI's ailment seldom vary. The men are always drunk and never use a condom, or if he did it broke. Their drippy dick contracted gonorrhea at Top Cham, Phan Rang, the Strip, Saigon, Nha Trang, Tuy Hoa, or R & R City, or any place on earth populated by prostitutes and infiltrated with soldiers.*

*All soldiers are supposed to be indoctrinated by their military commanders to use protective measures to avoid V.D. But in their moment of youthful, lustful, enormous urge—aggravated by the frustrations of Army life—all ability to reason is lost and only one thought is paramount to the priapic soldier: "to get a piece of pussy." Heterosexual soldiers talk about it every waking hour and dream of it at night, but I doubt if they will write their girlfriend or mother back home about contracting V.D. in defense of God and Country.*

*When the GI receives a pass to go to the village or the Strip, he has but one magnificent obsession: sex. It is for sale for the* *mere price of 200-400 piasters ($2-$4) or a pack of cigarettes, hairspray, or insect repellent. If it is near the end of the month and the soldier is broke, he can charge it. If he has unprotected sex, the chances are he will get a case of gonorrhea, syphilis, chancroid, venereal warts or multiple combinations thereof, and possible future complications of urethral strictures, circulatory and nervous disorders, pain, and sterility. The 18-year-old combat soldier doesn't think of the consequences of his insalubrious sex. He lives by the motto: "Eat, drink and be merry, for tomorrow we may die."*

*After sick call is over, it is lunchtime. It takes 5-10 minutes to round up Jim, Marv, Gene, and Ron into the jeep to go to the officer's mess, which is located in two tents a short five-minute drive from our dispensary.*

*Once a week we take the pill (chloroquine and primaquine phosphate) to minimize our chance of contracting malaria. At the entrance of the mess tent, I swallowed the bitter-tasting tablet and signed the sheet verifying that I received it, which is supposed to kill mosquito parasites in the liver and bloodstream.*

*The mess food is okay, considering the limited kitchen equipment they have. The salad bar has the standard fare—fresh lettuce, tomatoes, carrots, and cucumbers. Today, following the salad, we were served fresh hot rolls, hamburgers, potatoes, and mustard greens, which the mess sergeant had personally picked on a nearby mountain under military guard protection. Dessert was strawberry shortcake with coffee.*

*Sometimes I'm guilty of complaining about the food but rarely thanking the mess sergeant. Today I made the exception and thanked him for the extra effort to add the fresh greens.*

*After lunch, I return to my tent, remove my military gear, replace it with Bermuda shorts, and retire under the tropical sun for the afternoon. If a soldier comes by the dispensary in the afternoon, he is told to come back during sick call unless circumstances indicate that he can't wait until the next morning. This routine has resulted in the best suntan of my life. I read or do nothing until late afternoon, when I take a shower before going to supper.*

*Supper tonight was a break from the routine. Someone had*

*talked the mess sergeant into a cookout with baked beans, potato salad, and steaks. We brought the charcoal, which was locally produced, and placed it in a barrel cut in half and covered with a steel wire grid. He prepared 50 steaks for the 25 of us, which was more than enough.*

*Beer flowed freely before, during, and after supper. Everyone was in the "slap-on-the-back-jolly-good-I'm-your-buddy" mood. For me it was all so phony and all so common among a group of military men. Or maybe it was genuine, and I was the fake one, hiding my sexuality and unable to have an honest buddy conversation.*

*Since I was the only officer not drinking, I drove us back to the dispensary where I learned that several of our enlisted men had been to the village on pass this afternoon and returned with their sexual appetites satisfied—or so I assumed from their boasting. Two of the men had paid for hair perms and silk smoking jackets. And Gregory, our dispensary's 32-year-old beer-bellied dullard corpsman and veteran from the Korean War, returned from the village appearing exhausted from his sexual exploits. I am trying to suppress a mental picture of him in the whorehouse sweating profusely with his dog tags swinging back and forth on his neck as he grunts like an animal. He said he doesn't use a condom; instead he washes himself carefully afterwards. Our docs tried to explain to him that washing does not prevent V.D., but with inexorable certainty Gregory is not convinced to change his ways.*

*It is late and things have quieted down somewhat. The drinking has stopped and talking coming from the tents is subdued. The vulgar, revolting, boisterous whorehouse stories have ceased.*

*I spray the repellent into the mosquito netting hanging from the frame over my cot, and wait for a minute before pulling back the mosquito netting, brush the red dust off my green, quilted poncho lining, which serves as a blanket, and crawl into bed. After reading my Bible and attempting to reflect on the events of the day, I thank God that another day safely passed in the Nam.*

As I read this journal entry of my day, I feel guilty knowing that the majority of soldiers in Vietnam were not as lucky. There is no comparison between my typical day and a day with the 101st Airborne soldiers on a search-and-destroy combat mission walking through boggy rice paddies or sweltering, dense jungles. I slept on a cot in a tent, had three hot meals a day, and didn't risk my life; I provided support services for those guys who did.

In October, I was only working four hours a day, and another two months passed before I had equipment for my clinic and examined patients for the entire workday. Until then, I was violating the work ethic instilled in me by my parents. Also, I was not heeding the advice of the Apostle Paul to Timothy: "Work hard so you can present yourself to God and seek his approval."

Eventually I received clinic equipment and provided eyeglasses so that a soldier could better aim the barrel of his rifle at VC, who was waiting in the marshy rice paddies and the mountainous jungles to kill him. In very different ways, whether in combat or not, we were all a part of the war. Does this make me an accessory to killing Vietnamese? Or was I saving lives by improving our soldiers' vision so they could spot the enemy before the enemy could kill them? I convinced myself of the latter.

When I raised my hand to take the oath to defend my country, I had no idea it would lead me to Vietnam…and temporary work in an STD lab. Not my specialty training, but somebody had to do it, I guess.

# PORTULACA POWER

***7 October 1966***

*For a change of pace, I filled sandbags today, and I have the blisters on my right hand to prove it. Two of our dispensary's Vietnamese maids—Mia and Myh—helped me.*

*I used the sandbags to create a border for two flowerbeds—one on each side of the entrance to my tent. Tomorrow I am having a truckload of sand delivered from the beach to fill the flowerbeds. I will transplant beaucoup portulacas, which are growing in the wild outside our camp. Also known as rose moss, the portulaca blooms constantly and thrives in poor soil and drought conditions. Perfect.*

*Soldiers in my unit laughed at the idea of my planting flowers, but I have always loved flowers. In the summer, Grandma Reep always had flowers and ferns in clay pots on her porch. In late fall she and Grandpa would take the flowers to the "flower house"—a small rock house with a tin roof, windows facing south and a dirt floor to soak up the heat from the sun, which prevented the flowers from freezing during the winter. In the spring Grandpa Reep would move the ferns from the flower house to the porch, where he and Grandma would divide the large plants into two pots and fill them with rich barnyard dirt.*

*Granny Whitener also kept potted flowers and planted a row of gladiolus in the vegetable garden. She would cut these beautiful orange, white, and pink glads and bring them to church on Sunday to display in a basket behind the altar.*

*I am hoping that the portulacas' showy pink and white blossoms will add some color and life to my otherwise olive drab existence.*

*Instead of planting bright flowers, the enlisted men in our unit recently bought a beautifully colored parrot at the Phan Rang market. They spent time and energy to build a large cage for the bird and fed it primarily bananas. They named the parrot "Screaming Eagle," which is the official mascot of the 101st Airborne Division.*

*Last night the men attacked the parrot in an attempt to release their frustrations and anxieties. Perhaps they had problems back home, or were just bored. After a few beers one of the soldiers reportedly took the bird out of the cage and threw it on the ground as hard as he could. Another soldier threatened to demolish the next guy who hurt the bird. He then took the parrot outside and released it. The parrot did not return.*

*That a man in our unit would commit such a sadistic act unnerved me. It reminded me of an incident a few weeks earlier when a soldier trapped a live rat, doused it with petro and set it on fire. A small group gathered and laughed as the rat scurried, its body afire.*

*If war brings out the animal in men, I say, "Bring on the portulacas."*

I planted the portulacas in Vietnam not knowing that the same year "flower power" was in full bloom in San Francisco. Poet Allen Ginsberg coined the expression as a symbol of passive resistance to protest the war in Vietnam. Sometimes with flowers in their hair, hippies staged antiwar rallies as street theater. Inspired by the Beatles, white boys grew long, flowing hair. Black boys grew gigantic Afros as a symbol of Black Pride.

From San Francisco, flower power protests spread to New York City and the Pentagon in Washington, D.C. But the epicenter of flower power and its psychedelic music—Grace Slick and the Jefferson Airplane, Janis Joplin, the Grateful Dead—was the Haight

Ashbury district of San Francisco. It was a time when psychedelic art was on the album covers of many musicians, including Bob Dylan and the Beatles. Young people were breaking free from parental expectations and conventional lifestyles. It was a wild, wonderful, liberating time to be young in America.

My whole life had been about following the rules, and I was ready to experience freedom and grow my hair down—if not to my knees—at least to my shoulders. As soon as possible after my discharge from the army in 1973, I stopped cutting my hair and headed for the City by the Bay. By the time I arrived in San Francisco, I had missed the heyday of flower power, but the sexual revolution, which challenged social mores, was ongoing. And for gay men Polk Street was the happening place. We were visible everywhere in crowded bars and other businesses, which lined the street.

Through a friend I knew in the military, I met a man who rented me one half of his efficiency apartment on Pine Street—just one block from Polk. The apartment was tiny, but I spent little time there. By day I attended classes from the Free University (not free, but affordable) in stained glass, photography, macramé, and tennis, and at night I headed for the bars.

Come Sunday morning, I was at Cecil Williams' Glide Memorial United Methodist Church in the Tenderloin. It was church, as I never had experienced. Each service began with jazz music while brilliant orange, red, purple, and green light was projected onto the front of the sanctuary through a mixture of oil and water on a glass surface—a psychedelic experience without the drugs. Cecil, who was clad in his colorful dashiki and sporting a big Afro, appeared from the back of the sanctuary and proceeded to sashay down the aisle to the pulpit.

Williams was more than a showman; he was a compassionate man whose church welcomed all God's children—gays, hippies, the poor and marginalized people. (As a man of faith, he didn't hesitate to speak out against the corrupt Nixon administration. I remember his early prediction that Nixon would be forced out of office.) His mix of faith and politics gave me hope that I could be gay and acceptable to God.

After my year in Vietnam, where hiding my sexuality from others and myself was a matter of survival, I needed a safe harbor. I thrived in San Francisco—albeit for three short months—where being gay was normal.

It was a foggy Saturday morning in December when I stopped to give a ride to a skinny, young man on Polk Street. The cold wind blew his long straight, brown hair partially covering his face. I drove out of my way to take him to his destination. Before he got out of my car he said, "Man, can I have some change?"

"I have given you a ride, and you want money?" I angrily responded. I tossed him a dollar and said, "Get out." My utopian fantasy had ended.

# THE GOOD GUYS

***13 October 1966***

*Last evening three Military Police brought Buck Sergeant Pickett into our dispensary. Since early morning, Pickett had been drinking with his buddies who were preparing to leave the country. The MPs found him in a ditch, drunk, and his head bleeding. He was trying to fight the MPs with all his strength and was cursing every other word.*

*Drunk out of his mind, it took three MPs to hold him down while the Doc looked at the cut on his head. Pickett called Capt. Fishman everything except "doctor." After Doc cleaned the cut, applied a bandage, and gave him a tetanus shot, the MPs carried him to their jeep.*

*Today I learned more about Sgt. Pickett. He was recently in combat with a recon unit of the 327th Infantry Company in Dak To in the Central Highlands. Reportedly, the battle raged day and night leading to the defeat of the 24th North Vietnam Army. Pickett was awarded a Purple Heart and the Silver Star, a hero, who got drunk on his last day in the Nam.*

*The Silver Star—actually gold in color—is often given for leadership under fire, and is the third highest honor for heroism after the Distinguished Service Cross and the Medal of Honor.*

*Another 101st Airborne soldier, Capt. William "Bill" Carpenter—Commander of C Company, 502nd Parachute Infantry, 101st Airborne—gained notoriety four months ago when he supposedly called an air strike down on his own men. Carpenter—a 28-year-old father of three young children—is a former West Point Army football star. Two years earlier, in his first tour of Vietnam, he received a Silver Star.*

*In the battle with North Vietnamese forces in Dak To, Carpenter and his men lay in mud surrounded by the enemy; he thought they would be overrun. In a desperate move Carpenter called an air strike reasoning that he would take down the enemy with them. He said afterward that he might not have called in the strike had he known that napalm would be used. Seven of his men were burned from napalm, ten were killed and 33 were wounded, and he received his second Silver Star.*

*Capt. Brown, the Company Commander of A Company of the 502nd Infantry, 101st Airborne, was given the order to reinforce Carpenter—his former West Point classmate—who was surrounded by a Viet Cong battalion nearby. On June 10, 1966, Brown and his 170 men moved through darkness and treacherous terrain to the battle area. As his company reached the top of the mountain overlooking C Company, they received intense hostile fire.*

*Brown tossed a grenade behind the enemy's machine guns and shot two soldiers who ran toward him. While the rest of the company continued forward, Brown, who was under fire, maneuvered his company's machine guns into an effective position. As his unit reached the perimeter of C Company, the Viet Cong attacked the rear, seriously wounding one of his soldiers. Brown raced 30 meters down the slope to the wounded trooper and carried him to safety. He then assumed command of the perimeter and positioned his men to repel the repeated Viet Cong attacks. Throughout the next 30 hours, Brown continuously exposed himself to enemy fire as he carried ammunition, called in air strikes, and adjusted artillery fire. During a mortar attack he helped move wounded soldiers from exposed positions, and rallied his men to fight their way through the Viet Cong encirclement.*

*While transporting casualties over rough terrain to an evacuation point 1,000 meters away, Brown ordered a charge that overran the enemy's position. Although he was wounded with grenade shrapnel, he returned down the mountain to help his comrades carry the litter patients to the evacuation point. Brown received the Distinguished Service Cross for his heroism during the two-day battle.*

*I have thus far chosen not to record war stories, because I don't know the truth. I've talked with soldiers who convincingly tell of heroic acts, as well as monstrosities committed by our troops. I want to think of our troops as the good guys and the VC as the bad guys, who kill women and children, however, I believe that soldiers can succumb to the dirty deeds of war.*

Not only had I heard the story of Capt. Brown's heroism from his fellow officers, but it was also reported in *Time* magazine along with photographs, which depicted him firing an M79 grenade launcher and detonating a Claymore mine. The battle in the Central Highlands blends the actions of Brown and Carpenter because their forces consolidated and eventually broke out. The number of VC they and their troops killed varies with who is retelling the story.

In later years, Carpenter reportedly stated that he did not actually call the air strike directly on his position. Instead, he told the forward air controller to use the smoke marking his company's position as the aiming point for the air strike.

There were mixed reactions to Carpenter's decision to call in firepower. Some of his soldiers thought he overreacted while others believed that he saved their lives. As in most battles, it depends on where you were standing and where you were looking—and who is reporting the battle.

Commanding General William Westmoreland promoted Carpenter from his post as Commanding Officer of C Company to become his personal aide. Carpenter's Silver Star was later upgraded to the Distinguished Service Cross. In 1984, he went on to take command of the Combined Field Army in South Korea. He retired as a lieutenant general.

When Carpenter and Brown were in base camp, I shared meals in the same officers' mess and had conversations with them. I didn't think of them as either killers or heroes. Brown was a very personable guy, who seemed well on his way to a distinguished military career. I was surprised to later learn that he resigned his commission just two years after the battle in Dak To. He returned to the States, where he received a PhD in business administration from the University of California. He retired as the executive vice president of a consulting company.

The 502nd Infantry C Company had a reputation as one of the most effective—if not unconventional—companies within the second battalion. I heard that soldiers from Charlie Company carried tomahawks into battle until General Westmoreland ended the practice. After killing the enemy with his hatchet, a soldier reportedly cut off the head and brought it back as evidence of his deed in order to get a five-day R & R (rest and relaxation) trip, which he thought was his reward. The soldier was court-martialed and sent to Leavenworth, and the officer who issued the challenge to the troops was discharged. Was this a true story? Anything is possible in war.

Like most Americans who served in Vietnam, I will never forget the horrific story of My Lai. On March 16, 1968, a twenty-five-year-old platoon leader, Lt. William Calley, Jr., was charged with mass murder of unarmed women, men, and children in My Lai. Different versions of the massacre and subsequent cover-up by higher-ranking officers were revealed at Calley's court-martial.

The court-martial would never have occurred without the persistence of Spec. Ridenhour, a door gunner from the Aviation Section, and his pilot, Warrant Officer Honda, who flew over My Lai after the operation and observed a scene of complete destruction. Ridenhour had learned about the sordid events at My Lai secondhand from talking to soldiers who were there. He became convinced of a massacre of civilians and was so disturbed by the tales he heard that within three months of being discharged from the army he wrote a letter regarding his collected evidence to several senators, President Nixon, and Secretary of Defense Laird.

Senator Udall called for an official investigation, leading to trials that revealed the massacre and cover-up by senior officers.

A jury of his peers—six officers who had served in Vietnam—convicted Lt. Calley and sentenced him to life in prison on March 29, 1971, after he was found guilty of premeditated murder of twenty-two infants, children, women, and old men. The jury deliberated for thirteen days, and the court-martial decision was controversial.

I was outraged that only Calley—and none of his superior officers—was punished for the massacre and the subsequent cover-up. Two days after Calley's conviction, President Richard Nixon released him from armed custody at Fort Benning and put him under house arrest. He was freed three and a half years later.

We should always remember the My Lai Massacre. Our country sent eighteen-year-old young men to war armed with automatic rifles and grenades, and they obeyed the orders of a twenty-five-year old platoon officer. These warriors were trained to kill the enemy. They did...and more.

Today, the carnage continues in the tribal wars of Iraq and Afghanistan. The contempt and dehumanization of detainees occurred at Abu Ghraib, Iraq, where American soldiers tortured, raped, and murdered prisoners. In 2007, seven Marines were accused of killing civilians in Haditha, Iraq. None of the Marines accused received jail time.

I believe that Captains Brown and Carpenter were genuine heroes. Furthermore, I respect the difficult tasks of field soldiers and believe only a minority breach the laws of war. The fog of combat can temporarily blind young soldiers, but there have always been more good guys than bad ones. I blame the shameful acts of war on government policy makers, who should have never put our soldiers in harm's way in Vietnam, Afghanistan, or Iraq. All these wars were neither justified nor winnable.

# BAPTISM IN THE SOUTH CHINA SEA

***17 October 1966***

*It was a calm, clear, sunny Sunday morning. I drove to the nearby Air Force Officer's Club for breakfast. The wooden, upscale clubhouse provided a change of pace from the 101st Airborne's officers' club, which consists of two tents.*

*At 0900 I attended chapel services at the 101st tent chapel. The air was dry, and so was the sermon. Chaplain Reeves announced that there would be a baptismal service for three enlisted men in the South China Sea at 1115 today. I attended along with six other soldiers—two of which had M16 rifles to help protect us—and an MP who was on beach patrol nearby. I suppose it is not the first time that rifles have been present for a religious gathering, but it was the first time for me.*

*The soldiers who were about to be baptized wore their bathing suits and the chaplain who stood in water about waist high wore army fatigues. After the chaplain pronounced them baptized in the name of the Father, the Son, and the Holy Ghost, he lowered them backwards until their bodies were completely submerged in the South China Sea. It was a simple, short service.*

*Shortly after midnight—only about 12 hours since I was at the beach for the baptism—the VC attacked the fuel pumping station at the beach. The oil pipeline has been blown up three previous times in various sections. One of the 101st soldiers heard the explosion, went to investigate and was killed instantly by machine gun fire. The other two guards in the tent hit the ground but were wounded by shrapnel.*

*From baptismal service to a VC attack on the same beach, same day.*

Four years after the China Sea baptism, I stood on the banks of the River Jordan in the Holy Land. As I looked at the muddy water of this narrow river, I tried to visualize the story of the baptism of Jesus by John the Baptist.

My own baptism at age thirteen was by immersion—not in the sea or a river, but in a church sanctuary pool. The Church of God taught baptism by immersion, not the sprinkle of water, and not for infants. Although my parents didn't pressure me into baptism, it was expected. As I pinched my nose closed, my pastor placed one hand on my head and his arm around my waist as he gently pushed my head backward, completely submerging my body in the water. "In the name of the Father, Son, and Holy Ghost," he said as he quickly brought me back out of the water.

Recently the pastor at my church led a congregational ritual of remembering our baptisms. Dipping my hand into the baptismal bowl, I recalled my faith commitment to be a follower of Jesus and his teachings of love and forgiveness. My mind also wandered back to the three soldiers in the South China Sea so many years ago.

# CHICO AND THE MAN

***28 October 1966***

*Tonight I am in Penang, Malaysia. I flew from Nha Trang on a Pan American DC 6. Immediately after boarding, the stewardess gave us chilled pineapple juice followed by a cold towel for my face and hands. After takeoff we were served a steak dinner with all the trimmings and ice cream. The stewardesses, although very pleasant, were the oldest (all over 40) that I have ever seen working a flight.*

*Upon arrival at the Australian Air Force field on the mainland of Malaysia, soldiers briefly checked our shot records and ID cards. We then loaded onto buses, which were escorted through town to the ferryboat. It seemed strange to observe vehicles driven on the left side of the road. After a 30-minute ferry ride, in which we had time to convert American dollars to Malaysian dollars, we arrived on the island of Penang.*

*The population is a mix of Malays, Chinese, Indians, Japanese, and others. I saw Indian women wearing red and orange, green and gold sarees, which dazzled in the sunlight. The police wear khaki-colored short pants and black and white knee socks—probably from the British influence. Very smart looking.*

*I am staying at the Ambassador, which is a strikingly furnished,* *modern air-conditioned high-rise hotel. My room has a balcony, which overlooks the gay* streets, rooftops and mountains. As I looked down from the balcony, a kid began yelling, "Come down. I want to show you the city." I told him I wasn't interested, but later when I came out of the hotel he—along with a dozen other rickshaw boys—surrounded me, desiring my patronage. I told them I wanted to walk, but Chico, a kid who looks about 14 years old, followed me and insisted that I board his rickshaw.*

*Chico is a bright kid—turns out to be 17 years old—and speaks several languages. I asked him, "How long did you attend school?"*

*"Six months," he said. "I can learn everything I need to know without going to school."*

*Clearly, he can earn money without going to school. "You pay me what you want. If I show you number ten time, you don't pay me, but I will show you number one time. I will take care of you," he said.*

*He took me to two bars where I drank Coke and tea and talked to the girls. Chico told me that the girls in these bars don't "Boom Boom." (Need I explain the meaning?) "Girls from Vietnam have VD from buku GIs," according to Chico, who picked up the slang term from American soldiers.*

*Later in the evening, while eating at a restaurant, a local lady (perhaps the owner) came to my table and talked to me about everything from Charlie to LBJ's upcoming visit to Malaysia.*

*Chico took me to the waterfront. It began raining, so I returned to the hotel to bask in the luxury of a hot bath.*

***29 October 1966***

*When I awoke at 0800, I was actually cold from the air-conditioning. I walked out on my balcony, looked down and saw Chico lying in his rickshaw waiting for me.*

*The rickshaw, which Chico pedals like a bicycle, has a seat big enough for two passengers and is mounted on a frame supported by*

*Yes, I actually wrote the word "gay" to describe the streets. The word "gay" didn't enter the common vernacular as a descriptor for homosexuality until the 1970s.

*three wheels. (In Vietnam the rickshaw is known as a pedicab.)*

*The gentle rain was refreshing, but not conducive to sightseeing, so we went shopping. Most every clothing store has a wide selection of American-made clothes. The souvenir shops fascinated me with their fine wood, soapstone and ivory carvings, jade jewelry, and more. Salesmen latched on to me when I entered the shops, but I decided to shop around before making decisions. Enough of shopping, I was ready for sightseeing.*

*Chico took me by bus to the monkey village. The bus fare was cheap, and I enjoyed the ride as we passed by an upscale residential area of mansions. Monkey village—well, you guessed it—has thousands of monkeys which run loose in a jungle-like setting. I bought a bag of bananas, and the monkeys swarmed me, eating out of my hand. Before I realized what was happening, a local photographer began taking photos of me feeding the monkeys and then asked for $60 (Malaysian). I bargained for four copies of four photos for about five American dollars. Not bad.*

*The next stop was the Temple of the Buddhist Association. Upon entering the temple, I took off my shoes in order to walk on the sea of shimmering lotus-painted tiles. In the center of the building are three marble statues—Amitabh Buddha and his two disciples.*

*My cordial temple guide told me that the crystal chandeliers were imported from Czechoslovakia. The air was filled with the sweet smell of incense burning on the altar. For a small donation I looked through a magnifying glass at the small, cremated pieces of Buddha.*

*We continued by bus to the funicular railway at Penang Hill on the island of Penang. Built by the British in the early 19th century, the railway took us through rich green forests of tropical oak, tree ferns, and poinsettia plants to the top—more than 2000 feet above sea level. The panoramic view of George Town below surrounded by the sea and mountains in the distance did not disappoint.*

*It was long day of sightseeing, so Chico took me back to the hotel. Before leaving he asked me if I wanted to go out later to the bars. He offered many options—all of which I declined. Then he asked me if I liked boys. Quickly I said, "No!"*

*To avoid further inquiries, and at his insistence, I agreed for him to take me to a "special place."*

Chico was offering options, not only for bars, but also for sex. I panicked when he asked if I liked boys. Of course, I was intrigued by his offer but petrified by the possibility.

I wrote nothing in my journal about how the remainder of the evening unfolded. Although I wanted no record to remind me, I vividly remember that night. The "special place" was a brothel located in a nameless, nondescript building. In the reception room the madam greeted me and presented a book of photos from which I picked a photo of an attractive young girl. She led me to a tiny room—perhaps ten by six feet—just large enough for a twin-size bed. The madam told me that the girl, whom I selected, would be visiting me shortly. When she arrived some time later, she was not recognizable from the photo. This unattractive "girl" looked at least forty years old. Her facial features were sharp and her words hard.

After ten (or perhaps thirty) minutes of her futile attempts to turn me on, I got out of the bed, put on my clothes and was about to open the door. She puckered her blood-red painted lips into a snarl and spit out the words, "Go back to your mother."

I remained a virgin. Returning to my hotel room, full of guilt and self-hatred, I found a Gideon Bible on the bedside table and flipped through pages searching for solace.

I came upon Psalm 51 and David's words, "For I know my transgressions, and my sin is always before me. Against you, you only, have I sinned and done what is evil." David acknowledged his sin against God and offered a prayer for deep cleansing: "Wash me and I will be whiter than snow." I recalled those words from an old hymn I sang as a boy. I prayed for forgiveness and again promised God that I would not have sex before marriage. I felt pummeled by my carnal intent.

David prayed for joy to replace his misery, "Restore to me the joy of your salvation." I did not feel the joy, and I was miserable from the conflict of reconciling my Christian faith with my sexuality.

***30 October 1966***

*Today I encountered my first "Yankee, Go Home" sign in English, as well as Chinese letters. The Black Labor Party, whose stronghold is here in Penang, is demonstrating against President Johnson's visit to Malaysia—more specifically against the U.S. presence in Vietnam. Johnson will be in Kuala Lumpur today and tomorrow. According to the Malaysian edition of the* Sunday Times, *this is a "welcomed, friendly visit." The coverage in the newspapers is so favorable that it seems as if the President's Press Secretary, Bill Moyers, wrote the articles.*

*Traffic was tied up because of the overturned garbage cans, cement blocks, dead trees and other obstructive litter in the streets. Taxicabs were stopped in the midst of the crowds. Fortunately, Chico and I were on a crowded bus so the demonstrators did not notice the presence of an American. "If someone asks if you are American, tell them you are Canadian," Chico said.*

*Three trucks with policeman passed our bus; however, in the rough district where all the litter was tying up traffic, there was not one cop present. "Malaysian cops are number 10 because they don't fight like British and Australian policeman," Chico said. "British policemen don't need to carry pistols because they are tough, and the people respect them."*

*Great Britain and Australia have troops in Malaysia, but the British troops will be leaving next June while the Australian Air Force remains. The British troops are here because of the recent unrest in Indonesia.*

*The bus took us within walking distance of the Snake Temple. The temple was built around 1850 in honor of a Buddhist monk, Chor Soo Kong. Legend attributes healing powers to the Buddhist, who gave shelter to the snakes in the area.*

*Dozens of pit vipers were hanging everywhere in the temple, including the altar. The dense fog of incense burning is supposed to dope the snakes, and they did appear lethargic. Chico asked, "Can I take a photo of you with a viper around your neck?"*

*"Do you think I am crazy?" I said. But I couldn't resist the thrill and the opportunity to show off the photo. I agreed.*

I don't remember whether the viper felt cold when Chico draped the three-foot, greyish-brown snake around my neck, but I do remember my shock when the viper extended its tongue toward my face. Just as I reached over and pushed the head away from my face, Chico took a photo. The photo turned out blurry, but I clearly remember the scene. Perhaps the smoking incense did drug the viper, because I survived without a bite.

# SHAN POWERS

***30 October 1966***

*I took a taxi to the Penang airport where I boarded a Malaysian Airways flight to Singapore, with a brief stop in Kuala Lumpur. While on the ground, I saw signs welcoming President Johnson. I didn't see any demonstrators, but I was told that earlier in the day police killed a young man during a demonstration. I read that President Johnson was pleased with the Manila conference. "No new treaties were made, no new commitments were offered, but I can tell you now that I return more confident and hopeful than when I left," he was quoted in the* Stars and Stripes. *Propaganda... or wishful thinking?*

*At the Singapore airport I called the military R & R office, which sent a car to pick me up. Although the driver took me to several downtown hotels, I was not successful in finding a room. I had to settle for staying at the Sheffield House, which is leased by the U.S military. There are 100 sparsely furnished, air-conditioned rooms. It smelled and looked like a YMCA. The swimming pool, which has no lifeguard or rules, is open 24 hours a day. Soldiers and girls were either around the pool or streaming in and out of the guest rooms.*

*The Sheffield complex has a bookstore, camera and souvenir shop, clothing store, tourist office, barber shop, postal mail service, and restaurant, bar—all open from 0900 to 2100 hours. An advantage to shopping here, other than the convenient hours, is that the shopkeepers have contracts with the U.S. military, which prevents cheating the GIs. The self-contained complex is located in a gloomy slum area, but only a short distance from downtown.*

***31 October 1966***

*I walked to the Sheffield tourist office where Miss Koh, a tall, dark, beautiful woman in her 20s wearing a tight cheongsam (long Chinese dress with buttons down the right side of the dress), informed me that the bus tour I wanted was sold out. She offered to sell me a three-hour private car tour for three times the price of the bus tour. She could have talked me into most anything!**

*As I left her office she said, "Maybe we can talk some more tonight in the bar."*

*The private tour began with the Botanical Gardens, which consisted of acres of jungle, monkeys, and flowers—including a vivid collection of orchids. There were rubber trees transplanted from Brazil. I was told that rubber is now one of the leading exports of Malaysia.*

*The next stop was Tiger Balm Gardens—the Disneyland of the Orient. The park featured thousands of brightly colored cement or plaster statues depicting legends and traditions from Chinese mythology. (In 1937, the Aw brothers built the gardens to promote the Tiger Balm products produced by the family.)*

*At the Sakya Muni Gaza Temple I saw the magnificent 50-foot-high image of Lord Buddha, weighing 300 tons. A replica of a footprint left by Buddha on a mountain in Ceylon is carved in teakwood with mother of pearl inlay. For a small donation I was permitted to look at this unusual piece of art history.*

*Quite by accident in downtown Singapore, I witnessed an extraordinary religious street procession. A shirtless, penitent Hindu man dressed in bright yellow pants was dancing Kavadi, which incorporates physical burden and pain to seek help against*

* I was delusional and horny.

*the evil demon.*

*As the Kavadi bearer proceeded down the street surrounded by the cheering crowd, I saw three-foot metal spikes piercing his chest. The spears projected from a metal device covered in bright red fabric, which was fastened to his neck and waist. As he danced down the street, I saw blood oozing down his chest from the many wounds: his body resembled a living pincushion. My guide told me that the devotee would continue praying as the procession continued to the Temple.*

*After lunch I went to the swimming pool. As I was about to doze off, a 20-year-old attractive Chinese woman walked up to my lounge chair and introduced herself. Her name is Sanjo "Shan" Powers, and she was educated in an American school in Hong Kong, speaking and thinking like an American. She grew up in a foster home with British parents and now lives with an elderly lady. She attends college and works as a secretary part-time—or so she said.*

***1 November 1966***

*Shan and I went shopping. The merchants, who began with a price well above what they anticipated receiving, expected me to barter. I bought two transistor radios (one for Shan), a small tape recorder, another rosewood carving, a jade necklace and six yards of pale blue silk with gold embroidery for an Indian sari...or something. The shop clerk told me that the price was $65 (Malaysian dollars).*

*"I am not interested in buying six yards of silk," I said.*

*"So how much will you pay?" he asked.*

*"I'm not interested, but I will pay you $40."*

*"Impossible."*

*I bought the silk for $42, and I have no idea what I will do with it.*

*Tonight Shan and I went to dinner at the Goodwood Park Hotel, a fancy historic hotel built at the beginning of the 20th century as a club for the expatriate German community in Singapore. The hotel touts having the longest bar in Southeast Asia. Fifty years ago Anna Pavlova danced here, and in late 1939 the Duke of Windsor was a guest. During World War II when the Japanese occupied Singapore, the hotel became a residence for soldiers.*

*The food was forgettable, but the floorshow, which featured Las Vegas-style dancers and an old British comedian, was entertaining. After the show, the band played popular American songs. When they played "Strangers in the Night," the new release by Frank Sinatra, Shan said, "Let's dance."*

*"But, I can't dance," I pleaded, to no avail. We danced, or at least I moved my feet around the floor to the beat of the music.*

*Strangers in the night, indeed.*

The remainder of the night didn't make it to my journal, but…

We left the hotel and took a taxi to Shan's apartment. I got out of the cab and said good night. She paused and stared into my eyes for a moment. "Wait here," she said and hurried up the steps to her apartment. About five minutes later she returned to the cab with a small bag and said, "I'm ready now."

"Ready for what?" I asked.

"To spend the night with you."

"But I didn't ask you."

She looked at me with confusion registering on her face. "I don't understand. Come on, let's go."

I was dumbfounded. I just looked at her without speaking as she told the driver the address of Sheffield House.

"What is wrong with me?" she asked.

"Nothing is wrong with you." I didn't elaborate, but everything was "wrong" with me. Two nights ago I was with a prostitute. In the clamorous aftermath of that event, I had promised God that I wouldn't have sex until marriage.

We spent the night together. The earth didn't shake; the world didn't come to an end. The next morning I was just as confused, but I was not a virgin.

Once again I had strayed from the righteous path. The spirit was willing, but the flesh was weak.

I didn't plan the evolving events of that night. Shan was in charge, and she did not discuss birth control. I had never bought condoms, and we didn't discuss whether she was using birth control measures. (Birth control pills were not approved for sale in the U.S. until 1960 and were still illegal in Massachusetts until 1966.) When we parted the next morning, we did not exchange addresses. Since that night, I haven't had any contact with Shan.

Could I be a father, a grandfather? I think about the possibility. If Shan had a child, I am ineffably horrified that I was never part of his or her life.

# ELECTION VICTORIES

***9 November 1966***

*At last the Republican Party has come to life and won twenty-three governor's races. Lester Maddox, who closed down his restaurant rather than integrate it, won in Georgia. Ronald Reagan surprisingly won over incumbent Pat Brown in California. Reagan is an excellent speaker and has the personal magnetism of a Kennedy. His speech at the Republican convention in 1964 against government control of our society was tremendous. Governor Nelson Rockefeller won re-election for a third term in New York. Edward Brooke of Massachusetts became the first Negro elected to the Senate. In South Carolina, Strom Thurmond, a Democrat who turned Republican, easily won re-election.*

*On the Democrat side, it was no surprise that Lurleen Wallace, who ran as a stand-in for her segregationist husband Governor George Wallace, won in Alabama. U.S. Representative Basil Whitener (not a relative), who represents my district, was re-elected in North Carolina.*

*The only House election of interest to me was the defeat of Robert Bingham from North Carolina's 9th District to incumbent J .T. Broyhill of the Broyhill furniture family. I met Bingham when he toured Vietnam and stopped in Phan Rang. He fully supported*

*President Johnson's policy in Vietnam. Apparently the voters did not.*

*Unfortunately, I don't think my absentee ballot arrived in time to be counted. Since the majority of candidates I voted for lost, I guess it didn't matter in the final outcome.*

*I think a safe conclusion can be drawn that there were many dissatisfied voters with the present state of affairs. War, inflation, and the white "backlash" vote probably decided many races.*

You could probably say the same thing about the 2016 election. Add to those factors the endless war on terror, economic uncertainty, and racial inequality, which manifest in voters with fear, hatred, and misinformation.

The year 1964 was my first time voting in a presidential election, and I voted for Barry Goldwater. (If Goldwater were alive today, I don't think he would recognize the national Republican Party.) All my relatives on both sides of my parents' families traditionally voted exclusively for Republicans. My family's fundamentalist religion played into the conservative politics in the South. Other than tradition, I can't remember why I voted for Barry Goldwater.

The nomination of Hubert Humphrey versus Richard Nixon made it easier for me to break the family tradition and vote for a Democratic candidate. Nixon promised to bring "peace with honor" in Vietnam. (We know that didn't happen.) Two months before the 1968 election, Humphrey announced that, if elected, he would halt the U.S. bombing campaign in South Vietnam. Humphrey lost, and again I backed the losing candidate. I remember driving to the clinic the morning after the election and saying to myself, "The country deserves Nixon." Of course, we didn't.

My year in Vietnam radically changed my view about the role of government, political parties, and the future of our country. Our country was not infallible: We made a devastating decision to send troops to Vietnam to fight a civil war. I became more skeptical and cynical about the war and questioned blind patriotism and politics.

Today, I encounter patriotism at supermarkets, pet stores, and hardware stores. When I show my military ID at these stores, which give a discount to retired veterans, I am taken aback when the cashier says, "Thank you for your service to our country." The phrase unsaid by the cashier is "and I didn't have to serve." I don't expect to hear either phrase, and I realize that in many ways our society is grateful for the military.

I watch TV reporters wax rhapsodically over a soldier returning home at the airport to the open arms of a spouse and children: a frequent feature on local news. Why do I feel so cynical about the TV coverage of the returning soldier? I think it's because people glorify military men and women in uniform out of guilt for not serving themselves. Less than 1 percent of our society is now serving in the military. Only 7.3 percent of all living Americans have served in the military. There is no shared sense of sacrifice today as during World War II. And during the Vietnam War draft years, all strata of society served together. I believe in required military or civil service for all young people to share the sacrifice because of our country's endless wars. How about two years of service to our country for all eighteen-year-old men and women?

At my first duty station I remember the sound of the bugle playing retreat at 1700 hours, stopping whatever I was doing and paying respect for the flag. If I was driving, I got out of my car and stood at attention. During World War II, my Daddy said that seeing the American flag flying sent shivers down his spine. I shared his sentiment, but our ceaseless wars and lying government leaders have diminished my esteem for the flag.

Don't get me wrong. I love my country, but I don't wrap myself in the American flag. Today, the display of mindless red, white, and blue nationalism at the Republican and Democratic National Conventions, and other events, is repugnant to me. Does flag waving make one patriotic? How many of the rabid flag wavers and chanters would volunteer to go to war for our country?

The chant of "USA, USA, USA," whether at Republican or Democratic National Conventions, the Olympics, in our public schools, or even after the killing of Osama Bin Laden, strikes me as disgusting and arrogant when everyone knows that the USA is the most powerful country in the world.

Today's extreme nationalism has taken an ugly turn toward fear mongering against immigrants. America is a country built on immigrants, and I believe that we owe these immigrants the same welcoming arms that our ancestors received. Recently I was at our county's public library where I noticed a mom speaking Vietnamese to her two young sons. School is out, and instead of playing sports or video games, this mom had her kids in the library reading books. Each time she spoke to them in Vietnamese, they responded in perfect English. This family represents the America I love.

I recall the misguided nationalism of the 1960s and '70s when people equated support of the war in Vietnam with patriotism. If you didn't support the war, you were not patriotic. When I was stationed in Frankfurt, Germany, I saw an American car with the bumper sticker: "America, love it or leave it." Ironic, right?

In 2016, nationalism triumphantly returned to presidential politics with Donald Trump and his baseball cap slogan, " Make America Great Again," implying that the America of the past was greater than the America of today. Like the good old days of the 1950s? If you were white, male, Christian, and straight, America was great. I was there. I witnessed both our government and church organizations discriminating against black and gay people. I knew that discriminatory rules and laws applied to me.

Trump rose as a champion of white, working-class citizens by promising to restore their vision of America, and capitalizing on the feeling that the political establishment left them behind. His populist message is merely nationalism and racism intertwined: Make America Great Again—take us back to the time when white men held all the power and there was no threat of black, Hispanic, or Muslim people; stop immigration of non-whites and non-Christians; create fear of people who appear different from you.

I hope that we will not return to the 1950s, when racial discrimination and homophobia were not only tolerated, but also condoned. Our country survived the Civil War, the acrimony and social upheaval of the Vietnam era and George W. Bush. We will survive Trump (sing for us Gloria Gaynor!) until the next swing of the political pendulum toward a progressive society that values social equality, environmental protection, and public health.

I maintain hope, because there is no alternative.

# TURKISH DELIGHTS

***10 November 1966***

*To the lush music from the movie Exodus, one Turkish Delight draped in an almost transparent pale blue veil entered the outdoor stage and began dancing before a crowd of a hundred sex-starved GIs. She had long, black straight hair and was wearing a blue bra with silvery bangles, a blue billowy skirt that was split on the side to reveal her entire leg, and silver-colored high heels.*

*Her movements were a fusion of contemporary and Turkish belly dancing, which transitioned into sexual, pelvic thrusts. In a stream of flaming red gauzy material and flashing golden bangles, Delight Number two ran onto the stage. She threw herself down on her knees facing the audience and bent her upper body backwards until her head touched the stage. Her partially exposed ample breasts and wild hip thrusts left little to the imagination. Her facial expressions were provocative, and the troops reacted with screams of agony and delight.*

*The highlight of the show occurred when both "Delights" came down into the audience and used the long scarves hanging from their necks to pull two soldiers back on the stage. To my surprise one of the soldiers was Col. Abood, who began shaking his hips in an attempt to match the dancing gyrations of the Delights. The*

*101st Airborne troops roared their approval; clearly they loved seeing their leader dancing with the belly dancers. I felt like I was watching sex acts set to music.*

*After the Turkish Delight show, I walked to the 101st Officers' Club tent and watched the movie,* Zorba the Greek.

*My evening began with two women belly dancing in Vietnam and ended with two men dancing together in Greece—a real international night. I didn't like the belly dancing, but I loved the movie.*

Recently I watched Zorba the Greek again. I didn't remember the dialogue in the scene when the handsome Alan Bates requested Zorba to teach him to dance. As Anthony Quinn began to dance, he placed his left arm on the extended right arm of Alan Bates, looked him in the eyes and said, "I never loved a man more than you." Platonically, of course.

As I reflect on my condemnatory remarks about the Turkish Delights, I realize that I was an uptight person regarding anything of a sexual nature. At that time my condemnation of the Turkish belly dancing came from my moral values of what I perceived to be sinful. I believed that thrusting the pelvis in public was immoral—and this was ten years after the Ed Sullivan Show, where the cameras didn't go below Elvis' waist to reveal his sensual, pelvic thrusts. Just for the record, I was not an Elvis fan. I was a Pat Boone fan. I identified with Boone's wholesome, godly public image.

Four years after the Vietnam show, I enjoyed real Turkish delights—the candy—in Istanbul. It was Ahmet who first introduced me to the lokum treats, the delightful chewy mixture of honey, nuts, and dates covered in confectioner's sugar—and, to be perfectly honest, to other delicious treats as well.

In 1970, I flew from Frankfurt, my duty station, to Istanbul. There I met Ahmet, my idea of the handsome, mysterious Continental man. With a statuesque body and pale skin contrasting with striking, black shining hair, he could have been a fashion model. He became my very personal tour guide…and more. I returned for another visit and stayed with him and his retired father.

In 1971, Ahmet wrote:

> My sweet John, I am afraid of all things. The university is closed again because students are protesting the government and fighting with the police. I want to leave and go to Germany, but my father told me I must finish the university. Wait until December and I will come to you. We will be together. Be good. Be happy. I love you.

I didn't wait.

Recently I watched the TV coverage of another uprising in Istanbul and the attempted military coup to overthrow the government. I relived the sights, smells, and enigmatic energy of Istanbul. With its irresistible mix of Asian and European culture, Istanbul is the most fascinating city in the world. Mosques are everywhere, and the call to prayer is amplified, which make it difficult for even the non-believer to ignore. I was amazed at the intensity of the cobalt-blue tiles of the Hagia Sophia and the Blue Mosque. A boat ride on the Bosporus Strait, which links Turkey to the world via the Black Sea and Aegean Sea, provided an aquamarine backdrop to the Byzantine mosques and Ottoman palaces, which are forever etched into my memory.

Hundreds of shops in the ancient Grand Bazaar were redolent with tobacco smoke from water pipes (bongs), freshly ground spices, and strong, sweet coffee or tea served by merchants in small, gold-rimmed glasses. I wandered by stalls displaying brilliant fabrics and ceramics, hand-woven rugs and tiles, trinkets and junk. In the bazaar I bought a hand-painted green and blue ceramic water pipe—now a flower vase—and a brass samovar complete with teapot and eight gold etched serving glasses. Although both are now retired from service, I have used the bong and samovar to entertain guests.

Now as I write my thoughts turn to Ahmet and Turkish delights. We exchanged many letters, but never met again. Ahmet wanted to leave Turkey, because of the oppressive military government, and move to Germany. I hope he realized his dream.

I am grateful for the belly dancers, which were a catalyst for my interest in Turkey and led me to Ahmet and the delicious candy.

# RUSSIAN ROULETTE

***13 November 1966***

*Tonight I heard loud voices from the dispensary area. Apparently two sergeants had an ongoing feud—until tonight when one called the other out of the NCO Club and shot him in the leg with a .45 pistol. The wounded sergeant had lost a lot of blood but should be Okay. As the medevac landed, the chopper blades stirred up a storm of red dust, which covered my tent and cot. He was evacuated to the 8th Field Hospital in Nha Trang.*

*Soldiers are in Vietnam to kill or maim the enemy, not each other. But I was told by a company commander, who has led troops in battle, that he knows of several instances in which American soldiers have deliberately shot their own men in the back during battle. Afterwards these allegations are difficult to prove.*

*Last night a nineteen-year-old kid from the 101st Airborne killed himself accidently in a whorehouse near the beach. He picked up a .45 pistol that a friend was cleaning, pointed it to his head and said, "Look, man, I'm playing Russian roulette." An instant later he lay dead in a pool of blood on the table where our medic found him.*

*There are different versions of the story. One is that the dead kid didn't know the pistol was loaded. Another version was that he put one bullet in and spun the chamber. But there are unanswered questions. Why, for example, did the bullet enter his right temple when he was left-handed?*

I can't remember the investigation of 101st soldier's death. Whether his death was a homicide or the result of Russian roulette, it remains a tragedy.

As I reflect back on the death of the soldier, I am reminded of the Academy Award-winning movie *The Deer Hunter*, which was released some ten years later. The haunting movie is about male friendship, random violence, and the insanity of the Vietnam War. It vividly depicts the horrors of collateral damage. Three friends from a coal-mining town go to Vietnam, where they are captured and forced to play Russian roulette while their captors gamble on who will die first. Christopher Walken brilliantly played Nick, who stays behind after his friends return to the States. Eventually, the drug-addicted, crazed Nick plays Russian roulette professionally for money.

I cringed when I watched this mesmerizing scene, which became symbolic of the random, nonsensical, and dehumanizing violence of the war. I thank God that I was spared the battlefields of Vietnam and the resulting post-traumatic stress disorder (PTSD), which robbed many survivors of the ability to have a normal life.

While loss of life is tragic, soldiers who survived had to return to civilian life with the burden of battles still in their heads. This problem continues with our wars in Afghanistan and Iraq. I think of my bank teller who shared her 24-year-old son's story of the drug addiction he has fought since returning from two tours in Afghanistan. I saw the pain in her face as she told me that Cory has tried unsuccessfully to quit drugs and is waiting to be accepted in a VA Substance Use Disorder Treatment Program.

By God's grace, I didn't succumb to alcohol or drug abuse. I credit my strict religious upbringing and my parents' example in our home. I hope that soldiers, who suffer from PTSD, as well as drug or alcohol addiction, get the help needed to live meaningful lives. Our government owes them medical care, including mental health services.

# SHANKER

***17 November 1966***

*Shanker is dead. The black mongrel puppy of indeterminate breed habitually dug holes in my flowerbed outside my tent. His name, which reflects the humor of our corpsmen, is a reminder of the possible consequences of venereal disease. "Shanker" is slang for chancroid, a sexually transmitted disease which results in painful, open sores on the genitals.*

*Shanker was hit by a jeep in the road in front of our dispensary while having sex. The other dog died instantly, but Shanker lived for several hours. Frenchie, our X-Ray technician, determined that his skull was fractured and cerebral fluid was leaking from his nose. He was put to sleep forever. I shed no tears. He died the death of a lover—what a way to go!*

*Within a few hours our dispensary's enlisted men had found another mongrel dog and named him "Leg." (Anyone in our base camp that is non-airborne is referred to as "leg." For example, dispensary staff members are called "leg medics.") Leg has the bone structure to become a big dog. I plan to make friends with him while he's small and train him to stay out of my flowerbed.*

Even though I love dogs, I never had a connection to either Shanker or Leg. Neither of the mutts was among the nearly four thousand trained service dogs deployed to Vietnam. Although I never saw a military dog during my year in Vietnam, I know they were later assigned to guard the perimeter of the Phan Rang and Cam Ranh Air Bases. All U.S. military services deployed trained Dobermans, Labrador retrievers, German shepherds, and Belgian Malinois to serve in Vietnam. Using their sentry and scouting skills, the dogs were credited with saving thousands of servicemen.

So what happened to the trained dogs after the war? Considered surplus equipment, they were crated and left behind to be euthanized or turned over to the South Vietnamese forces. But these war heroes are not forgotten. There are War Dog Memorial statues at Fort Benning, Georgia, and New Jersey's Vietnam Veteran Memorial. In 2013, the national memorial to honor war dogs was opened at Lackland Air Force Base in San Antonio, Texas.

Since the Vietnam War, working dogs and their handlers continue to be trained at Lackland for deployment to Iraq and Afghanistan. Unfortunately, the U.S. military used unmuzzled working dogs to intimidate and bite prisoners during interrogations in Iraq. In spite of the Geneva Convention, similar disgraceful tactics were used in the Guantanamo prison. After photos of prisoners being tortured and sexually abused were aired on *60 Minutes* and published in the *New Yorker*, the Department of Defense prohibited the further use of dogs by U.S. forces in Iraq.

In 2011, Navy Seals used a Belgian Malinois named "Cairo" in Operation Neptune Spear, which killed Osama bin Laden.

When most of us think of military service to our country, I doubt that dogs come to mind. Certainly not Shanker and Leg. But dogs are war heroes, too, and I hope that military personnel treat them with respect after their valuable service to our country.

I didn't own a dog for years to come, but at the insistence of Tony (more about Tony later), we adopted Scarlett, a poodle who was born the day the U.S. invaded Iraq in 1991. Although I wanted a dog that didn't shed hair, I resisted owning a poodle, because I feared appearing as the stereotypical gay man walking a poodle in our neighborhood. But I got over it. We now have our third poodle,

Rusty. Each dog has been an individual with a distinct personality, just like Shanker and Leg.

# 101ST AIRBORNE

***22 November 1966***

*Upon arrival at the 101st Airborne Division's permanent base camp in Phan Rang, P-training (preparatory training) is given to all newcomers, a.k.a. "cherries." Although they are new soldiers in Vietnam, they have already successfully passed army basic training and graduated from jump school, where they earned their U.S. Army Parachutist Qualification wings.*

*As part of the orientation training, experienced 101st instructors share their lessons learned during five days of lectures, demonstrations, and firing various weapons, as well as a night course. Although the soldiers have previously been trained for battle situations, P-Training is a realistic orientation to Vietnam and its particular hazards. Physical training also helps the soldiers acclimate to the heat before going out to real field operations. Following the training, the soldiers will be sent for another week of jungle training in the mountains.*

*I attended P-Training this morning to check out the lectures and demonstrations. An NCO (noncommissioned officer) pitched the advantages of soldiers extending their tour beyond one year. If a soldier extends his tour for six months, he is given a free 30-day leave and plane fare home and back to Vietnam. I am not sure why this would be an adequate incentive. Not for me.*

*A military police sergeant explained the rules and regulations that applied to the men on post. Curfew is 1800 hours to return from the village, beach or the Strip. No weapons can be carried in the village.*

*We moved to a wide-open field for the next lecture and demonstration. A 30-something, trim, muscular sergeant told us about the tactics used by the Viet Cong. He described a VC as a 90-pound, underfed, poorly equipped, malaria-infested peasant. A soldier dressed in black pajamas, sandals and a straw hat interrupted the sergeant. The actor VC proceeded to expound on the merits of the North Vietnamese soldier and the VC fighter. "Although the VC is small in stature and poorly equipped, don't ever underestimate our ability and determination to kill Americans," he said. He vividly demonstrated the art of camouflage when suddenly a VC comrade jumped from a hole a few feet from us. If he had been a real VC, several of us could have been killed before we realized what had happened.*

*The VC sergeant pointed out that he never fights unless he has the advantage in manpower and weapons. The exception is when he is guarding precious supplies such as food, ammunition or medical supplies. His tactic is to harass American troops with sniper fire while his troops wait until a day when they can outnumber and outsmart the enemy. He is an expert when it comes to ambush and booby traps. Old men, women, and children sympathetic to the communist cause make sharp, barbed bamboo pungi stakes, which are covered with human excretion or poison. These are hidden in tall elephant grass or rice paddies. When stepped on, these poisoned stakes can kill an American soldier within hours if he does not receive treatment.*

*The VC steals Claymore mines and collects scrap metal discarded by Americans to reuse. In the jungle the VC use a vine to string together grenades set up to be tripped when a soldier cuts or trips on the vine. The result is a chain reaction of explosions that kill American soldiers. An innocent-looking farmer working in a rice paddy, who waves to you as you pass on the road, may be the one who cuts your throat the same night. A patient farmer may sit in the jungle near a road for a week watching for an American truck to pass so he can detonate a mine buried in the middle of the road. The VC actor ended by stating, "I will be waiting for you in the jungle."*

*I couldn't help wondering how many of the group of 30 soldiers in this P-Training class would not live to return to Phan Rang for out processing, and how many would be injured or become ill from malaria. Only time will tell.*

*Tonight the steaks and liquor were abundant in quantity and quality as our dispensary staff hosted a party for the 101st Airborne Headquarter officers. The steaks were prepared teriyaki style with beer, soy sauce and garlic by Capt. Honjo, who is from Hawaii, a.k.a. "Pineapple."*

*Maj. Scott played the guitar, and we sang on and off (between steaks) for most of the evening. Others watched skin flicks. Instead of watching porno, I went to my tent to read.*

*Much later in the evening Scott sent someone to get the "optometer doctor" to sing with him. I returned to what was left of the party scene, sang with him and ate another steak. Around midnight everyone had left except Scott, who was still eating, drinking and singing "500 Miles" and "Jamaica Farewell" into the wee hours of the morning.*

The 101st Airborne has a proud history going back to D-Day landing in Normandy during World War II, and continuing in Vietnam and later in Iraq. The 1st Brigade of the 101st Airborne Division arrived one year before (1965) our dispensary moved to Phan Rang. Most of the soldiers were sent to the mountainous jungles of the Central Highlands, and over the course of the Vietnam War the division suffered almost twenty thousand soldiers killed or wounded. Of the thirty soldiers taking the training that day, I know at least one of them died, because his new military glasses, which I made for him and sent forward to his field assignment, were returned to me and the package was stamped "deceased."

On January 15, 1991, the 101st fired the first shots of Operation

Desert Storm/Desert Shield, destroying Iraqi radar sites. They went on to secure Iraqi territory in the Euphrates River Valley, enabling other U.S. forces to attack in Kuwait. The 101st soldiers were back home by May 1, 1991.

Because of the Iraqi War, my coincidental history with the 101st Airborne Division continued as I was called back to active duty for medical support at Walter Reed Medical Center in Washington, D.C. I was discharged from active duty and returned to my reserve unit on May 15, 1991. Both the 101st soldiers and I served the same time period in Operation Desert Storm.

From time to time I am asked what the war was like. Whether responding to the Vietnam War or Desert Storm, the answer is the same: The 101st soldiers fought on the battlefields while I provided medical support at a safe distance. During both wars, I knew that the military could discharge me for my sexual orientation, but I did my job and kept my head down. My luck continued.

# THANKSGIVING DAY

***24 November 1966***

*Our dispensary was closed today except for emergencies, one of which occurred at 0630 when a young soldier jumped on top of our ambulance and wouldn't come down. When asked what would bring him down from the ambulance he replied, "A cup of water." After receiving the water he ceremoniously blessed it in the name of the Father, Son and Holy Ghost, drank it and came down. He wanted to discuss religion, but was completely irrational. Our doc gave him a strong sedative. This is not the first mental patient we have had at the clinic.*

*After sleeping later than usual, I spent the remainder of the morning lazily. The highlight was pitching a couple games of horseshoes; I lost. Around 1130 hours Gene, Marvin, Jim, Ron, and I got into the jeep and went to the mess hall where they served the official international U.S. military Thanksgiving Day menu—shrimp cocktail, roast turkey, gravy, dressing, creamed corn, potatoes, glazed sweet potatoes, cranberry sauce, relishes, Parker House rolls, pumpkin pie, mincemeat pie, fruit cake, nuts, candy, tea, lemonade and coffee. It is amazing how our cooks can pull off this traditional feast thousands of miles from home.*

*General W. C. Westmoreland, commanding officer of Vietnam, sent us the following message:*

> *This Thanksgiving Day we find ourselves in a foreign land assisting in the defense of the rights of free men. On this day we should offer our gratitude for the abundant life, which we and our loved ones have been provided. May we each pray for continued blessings and guidance upon our endeavors to assist the Vietnamese people in their struggle to attain an everlasting peace within a free society.*

I had much to thank God for, but not for being in Vietnam on that Thanksgiving Day. I was becoming increasingly disillusioned with the purpose of American troops fighting in Vietnam. I didn't agree with Westmoreland that Americans were "assisting the Vietnamese people in their struggle to attain an everlasting peace." Four months into my tour of duty I was struggling to find a single positive example of how the American troops had improved the life of the Vietnamese people.

Fifty years later, I still struggle to list any positive outcome. The death toll estimates are staggering: 125,000 to 495,000 North and South Vietnamese civilians, over one million North Vietnamese and Viet Cong fighters, over 200,000 South Vietnamese soldiers, 58,200 U.S. Armed Forces, 4,000 South Koreans, 350 Thais, 500 Australians, and 36 New Zealanders.

On the morning of April 30, 1975, South Vietnam's President Duong Van Minh surrendered to the Viet Cong and the last U.S. marine left Saigon. (President Minh had been sworn in only two days prior to his announcement.) His predecessor, Nguyen Van Thieu, had resigned the previous week—the same Lieutenant General Thieu, who was elected in the September 1966 election.

Our military abandoned thousands of Vietnamese civilians, who worked for the U.S. Government, as well as all the base camps, ports, airstrips, hospitals, storage depots, and construction equipment scattered all over southern Vietnam. Two years later North and South Vietnam were united as the Socialist Republic of Vietnam—a Communist government.

After the war, thousands of Vietnamese sympathetic to the U.S. were executed and over one million sent to prison re-education camps. The boat people, who left their country and were fortunate enough to survive the deadly seas in small boats, became refugees. The U.S. accepted over 800,000 refugees, England 19,000, France 96,000, Australia and Canada 137,000.

Two decades after the fall of Saigon, President Clinton, who as a young person opposed the Vietnam War, re-established official recognition of Vietnam. Just as the Vietnam War was good for big business, the recognition of Vietnam is good for American business. In 2014, the two countries traded more than 35 billion dollars in goods. Thanks to the war, the U.S. is the largest export market for Vietnam.

Money and war. And the beat goes on...and on.

# RELIGIOUS BELIEFS

***27 November 1966***

*About thirty minutes before leaving for Bible study I was sitting in my office reading when I overheard an enlightening, disturbing conversation among the patients in the ward.*

*My office and clinic are carved out of the larger space in the Quonset hut, which is also used as a patient ward. The plywood walls separating my clinic from the ward are paper-thin, so it was easy to hear the conversation on the other side. I have left out most of the curse words, which were used in every sentence, but here's the gist of the conversation:*

*Joe: My old man and woman are real religious. They read the Bible all the time, but they never work together when they speak in tongues. When I was three years old, a preacher called me up to the front of the church and said to the whole congregation, "This here is Brother Brown's boy, and he's going to be a preacher when he grows up." I never will forget that.*

*Jim: My church says a girl can't wear jewelry, makeup, short skirts and all that stuff, right? Well, my wife was religious like that until I tarnished her fuckin' brain. (Laughter from all.) I taught her how to dress, and now she wears short skirts and all that stuff to church with me. People just turn around and stare.*

*Jack: You know the church in the army ain't got no religion. They don't preach the real Christ, and the chaplains tell dirty jokes and try to be one of the guys. I don't have no respect for a chaplain that talks that way to guys.*

*Joe: I took several years of Bible study in school. It never did me no good. I just took it because there were a lot of good-looking chicks in the class. (Laughter.)*

*Jack: At least he is honest.*

*Jim: My mother wrote me a letter and asked me to read the 91st Psalm.*

*Jack: Have you read it?*

*Jim: No. Anybody got a Bible?*

*Joe: Yeah, I'll read it. "He who dwells in the shelter of the Most High, who abides in the shadow of the Almighty, will say to the Lord, my refuge and my fortress; my God in whom I trust. For He will deliver you from the snare of the fowler."*

*Jack: That's good for over here, but you gotta practice it.*

*Jim: I had a buddy who carried his Bible in his shirt pocket. He said that some day it would save his life, but he was shot in the other side of his chest.*

*And so the conversation went on and on. Two of the three soldiers were sons of preachers. It disturbed me that they only remembered negative aspects of religion—the "can't" and "don't" issues. No wonder that young people drift away from the church as soon as they have an opportunity.*

*It got me thinking. Should I be basing my spiritual life on negative teachings? How do religious beliefs (or lack of them) translate into daily life? I have begun to question everything that I once held as sacred and established truth. I am searching for answers.*

*Since I was two weeks old, I have regularly attended church. In fact, the church community was the center of our family's social and spiritual life. I accepted church teachings without questioning. I had a good upbringing, and I am thankful I was raised in a loving, Christian home. I desire the same for my children.*

*Now for the first time in my life I have had free time to think for myself with no outside pressure from family or friends. In order to be a true Christian, is it necessary to blindly accept traditional biblical teachings? Are values constant? What is truth? Does situational morality exist? What is the basis for judging right and wrong?*

*What shook up my thinking was reading* Psychoanalysis and Religion *by Erich Fromm, who points out the reasons why people accept religion. A search for a higher being is inherent in humans; however, people satisfy this longing to serve their God in various ways. He revealed how we use religion to fill the gap in our deficient personality. Instead of thinking "God is punishing me" perhaps it is one's own stupidity at fault. He proposes that we should take responsibility for our actions rather than choosing to leave results to God. Many of his ideas make sense to me.*

*My orderly world of good and evil has been shattered in Vietnam. I periodically stop praying and reading the Bible because it seems futile and artificial. I resumed Bible study and chapel services, but only as a ritual. I am losing touch with God. How can I pray to a God whose very existence I now question? I have never been in this state of mind, and it scares me.*

*Last night I talked to my friend, Lt. Ken Cohen, about his religious beliefs. Regarding morality, he believes that an act becomes immoral when one refuses to accept responsibility for it. Ken continues to question the existence of God, but has not come up with all the answers. "But this is good, because this is a sign of a growing, intelligent person," he said.*

*Not only did I search for answers from Ken, but also from Capt. Joe Martin, whom I met at Bible study on the ship. I wrote Joe, who is stationed in Saigon, asking many of the same questions. He responded, "I sympathize greatly with your concerns but although this is of little consolation and from one who is in the same predicament, I think we can find some reassurance in the old adage: Who never doubted never half believed."*

*Although it was of little comfort, I was not alone in my questioning.*

My earliest memories of church are singing in the choir (my Daddy was the director), playing my accordion for prelude to worship (favorite medley was "My Jesus I Love Thee" and "Sweet Hour of Prayer"), and praying on my knees (without kneelers for comfort). In the beginning, our country church was without indoor plumbing or central heating; a pot-bellied stove kept us warm in the winter. The brothers and sisters of the church were a community of hard-working, God-fearing, tithing, good people, who worshiped and socialized together. On Wednesday night, scripture was read, and people testified about the goodness of the Lord, requested prayer and then we all (if able) knelt and prayed, using the wooden benches to prop our elbows to hold our bowed head. I prayed on Wednesday night and throughout the week. At home we prayed before each meal and at night before going to bed. I prayed to Jesus—imagining Sallman's painting, The Head of Christ, as a handsome man with long flowing brown hair and beard. (He doesn't look Middle Eastern at all.)

The fundamentalist, evangelical church of my youth was based upon a judgmental religion of strict rules: no smoking, divorce, drinking alcohol, dancing, playing cards, attending movies. Of course, there could be no sex outside of marriage. If or when I broke the rules, I sinned, and without repentance I would go to hell. I remember evangelists at revival meetings vividly depicting hell as consumed by fire and brimstone—eternal damnation by God.

I couldn't easily give up my religious beliefs because from my earliest memories, I was indoctrinated. I didn't challenge the inspired supremacy of scripture. My Daddy believed in the Hebrew scripture from Proverbs: "Teach children how they should live, and they will remember it all their life." He was right. I bought into church doctrine without a struggle. It was not a conscious decision, no debate. My parents consistently "talked the talk and walked the walk." Their church values were my values and reinforced three times a week in worship services. I was among the righteous, forsaking worldly pleasures, especially of the flesh. We would be rewarded in heaven for being faithful to church teachings. When my faith wavered, I prayed. Or sang gospel songs in my head.

Vietnam offered me breathing space to break free of my church and family's expectations and assumptions. The questioning of my relationship to God and church doctrine should have begun years earlier when I recognized my attraction to boys, but I was taught that homosexuality was a sin and not compatible with being a Christian. Since I wanted to be a Christian, I suppressed my homosexuality, dated women, and prayed for God to change me. A tug-of-war played out inside my head. I repeatedly asked forgiveness for my carnal thoughts, which left me overwhelmingly guilty.

In Vietnam I recorded a tape cassette for my parents to reassure them of my well-being. I talked about everyday life in the Nam and then concluded by singing, "His eye is on the sparrow and I know He watches over me." Reassuring. But then came the verse, " I sing because I'm happy, I sing because I'm free." I was not happy. I was not free.

During my first year back to the States from Vietnam, I temporarily pushed conflicting thoughts about sexuality and religion into a recessed, dark corner of my mind. I was spiritually adrift. As I began dating men, I convinced myself that I could lead two separate lives: one as a straight, churchgoing soldier, and the other as a man who dated men.

I wanted religious anonymity, so I attended an urban Baptist church where few people knew my name, and I could be lost in the crowds each Sunday. I didn't want family and friends to ask personal questions, so I kept everyone in my life at a safe distance. I couldn't figure out how to reconcile Christianity with my life.

In 1968, I welcomed military orders to Germany, but I couldn't easily abandon or escape my religious upbringing. At Lundstuhl General Hospital, I attended chapel services, which led to singing in the choir and dating a chaplain's daughter. I was also youth leader, responsible for Sunday evening youth meetings and occasionally off-base trips.

The following year I moved to the big city of Frankfurt, where I met Karlheinz, who became my first long-term boyfriend. I stopped going to chapel, because I could no longer conform my sexuality to organized religion. I couldn't reconcile loving Karlheinz and a loving God, whom I believed condemned our relationship. Why should I pray or attend church to worship?

On and off over the years, I visited numerous Protestant churches, from Episcopalian to Unitarian, but I didn't attend church regularly. Not until 2002, when I attended First Congregational United Church of Christ in Asheville, North Carolina, did I feel like I had come home. Unlike the Apostle Paul on the road to Damascus, I did not fall down on my knees or experience a brilliant light from heaven, but from singing the first hymn I sensed the peace of God in my heart.

I was impressed that the church had just completed a year's process to become an opening and affirming church for gay and lesbian congregants. Within a year I was asked to help teach Sunday school in the kindergarten class. I was overwhelmed by their trust and without hesitation said, "yes."

My early religious experiences within the fundamentalism of my hometown church shaped my character and colored all my life choices, while holding me captive for over 40 years with the hammer of guilt—never good enough, never measuring up to a holy and blameless life. While I moved beyond those asphyxiating beliefs, I recognize that those church traditions helped make me the person I am today. I no longer fear that my sexuality and spirituality are incompatible. I remember the words of an old spiritual: "And my soul looked back and wondered, how I got over Lord." Yes, by the grace of God, I got over.

Recently, I asked my nephew, a chaplain in the Air Force, about the diversity of religious beliefs in the military today. "We have chaplains representing all the major faiths: Catholic, Protestant, Jewish, Islamic, and Wicca with weekly services on base."

"Wicca?" I shook my head in disbelief.

"Yes, Wicca services every Sunday morning at 9 a.m."

"If I can't help the person who comes to me for pastoral counseling," he continued, "I can refer him or her to another chaplain who can. When gay couples come to me to be married, I can't perform the marriage because the Church of God, which commissioned me to be a minister, forbids it. If I went against the church teaching, I would lose my commission. But I can refer the couple to a United Church of Christ chaplain, and she can marry them."

Thanks be to God for the United Church of Christ!

I wrote in my diary about the desire to have a "Christian home for my children." As it turned out, I never had children, but in 2007 at the Santa Maria Reina Catholic Church, Mexico City, Tony and I became official godparents at the baptism of Camila Lomeli, Tony's niece. According to the official Catholic canon, two people of the same gender cannot be godparents and both must be Catholic. The priest ignored both of those rules. As I sat in the modern-designed Santa Maria Reina, I looked at the front of the church beyond the pulpit through a high-vaulted glass wall to a garden overflowing with fuchsia bougainvillea. A bare, cement cross was suspended from the ceiling against the glass.

I couldn't believe that I—a gay Protestant Christian—was being designated as an official godparent in a Catholic church. The priest charged Tony and me with Camila's spiritual guardianship—a responsibility that I take seriously. I thanked God for the opportunity.

# THE BIG LIE

***1 December 1966***

*The clinical equipment, which I packed in Ft. Lewis in June, has never arrived. But thanks to a medic in the 48th Aviation Company, I have a retinoscope, ophthalmoscope, a tangent screen, perimeter, numerous charts and a small set of trial lenses. He discovered the unused equipment in boxes stored in a nearby flight surgeon's office. After nearly a six-month hiatus, my clinic is completely functional, and I am gratified to examine patients again. Working all day helps pass time.*

*A week ago Sara, a Red Cross recreational worker and former high school English teacher, came in for a vision exam and new glasses. Sara has been in Vietnam for four months and although she realizes the error of her ways, she will probably stick it out for the complete year's tour. She is wearing an engagement ring and came to Vietnam "to think things out." Unlike soldiers, she could resign at any time and go home. She came for an eye consult because the constant dust here is interfering with wearing contact lenses. She asked me to order her glasses, which is against regulations, because only soldiers are entitled to military eyeglasses. I lied by ordering her military glasses as "Sam Yapel, PFC, age 23."*

*Today Sara came by the clinic and picked up her new glasses.*

*She was thrilled to see clearly again and danced up and down. I didn't tell her the moniker given the ugly tobacco-colored eyeglass frame: birth control glasses, because no one would have sex with anyone who wears them.*

We lie. We lie in marriage, in business, to avoid hurt feelings, or to keep a job. Lying politicians call it "alternative facts." Our government lied about enemy body counts, escalation of the war, and bombing the North Vietnamese Army into submission, all adding up to the big lie—we were winning the war in Vietnam.

I didn't lie to swindle or boast. I lied to the military so that I could order eyeglasses for Sara. Although I never accepted lying as normal, I believed that the lie for eyeglasses was justified. Small stuff compared to big lies.

I lied on the military induction health form, and I lied to myself throughout my year in Vietnam. In my heart I knew I was homosexual, but I somehow believed that I could change. I repented to God and asked to change…over and over.

Although I lied about my sexuality, I still drew other moral lines—rejecting pornography, sex with local prostitutes, and alcohol. Being a teetotaler was a choice, and slowly I changed. Two years after Vietnam, while stationed in Germany, I drank my first bottle of beer. Drinking wine was an easy choice—after all Jesus made wine.

Being located in Germany—away from family, church, and societal constraints—gave me the freedom to love and be loved by a man. It was an incomplete freedom, as I felt compelled to meet military expectations by intermittently dating women for official military functions for three more years. I am truly sorry for the dishonest relationships during this time with Claudia, Sharon, Lea, Rachael, and Ilene, not to mention other women whose faces are clear in my mind, but whose names I can't recall.

When I was about ten years old, I attended a Sunday school class taught by my Granny Whitener. Granny was a tall, big-boned, big-love godly woman with short silver-gray hair styled in finger waves. In her booming voice she called me to the front of the class and asked me to sit on a wooden chair while she wrapped one string around my chest and upper arms and tied it. "The string represents telling one lie," she said. "Can you get out of it?"

"Of course, I can," I replied as I moved my arms, easily breaking the string. She continued to tie multiple strings around me until I couldn't move my arms.

"Now can you break out?" she asked. I tried my best to break free, but I couldn't. I was caught in a string of lies.

Granny had made her point.

But years later I wanted a military career, so I chose to be dishonest about my sexuality. Lies, lies, and more lies. The noose tightened. The struggle continued.

# NO PLACE FOR A LADY

***4 December 1966***

*Last night the 101st Airborne Support Club gave a farewell party for men in the Air Force Flying Squadron. We had grilled steaks, chicken, baked beans, potato salad, deviled eggs, stuffed celery, tomatoes, and rolls. As we were eating, the men in the adjacent bar began singing dirty limericks and perverted renditions of Christmas songs.*

*Almost all the men broke up in fits of laughter as the songs became raunchier. From "Twelve Days of Christmas" to improvised scripture—nothing was off limits. Sara (the Red Cross girl whose glasses I made), sitting at a table near me, nervously laughed during the songs.*

*Tonight while we were eating supper in our mess tent, the men started singing their version of "The Twelve Nights of Christmas," which they had learned the previous night. Sara was eating supper with us again and became quite upset. After she finished the meal, she stood up from the table and made a brief speech.*

*"I am sorry if my presence hampered your fun. You should have respect for a lady. Last night I was kept awake by the dirty songs and now you are repeating the same stuff again." (The Red Cross sleeping tent is only 50 yards from the 101st Club.)*

*She walked out of the mess hall, and I thought: War is no place for a lady.*

I met only two of the over six hundred young, college-educated Red Cross women to serve in Vietnam. Their uniform was a pale blue dress cut a few inches above the knee, with Red Cross insignia on the dress collar and a name tag on the right side. I don't remember the women wearing pants, but surely they did when they visited troops in the field.

The Red Cross women began arriving in Vietnam the year before I arrived, and left when our soldiers were withdrawn in 1972. Their nickname "donut dollies" came from World War II when the Red Cross women were known for providing donuts and coffee for servicemen. I never saw a donut during my year in Vietnam.

Red Cross women staffed recreational centers, visited troops in the hospital, and handled over two million emergency communication services between soldiers and families back home. There was no telephone access for troops in the field, so the women handled notifications from families to soldiers and made arrangements for emergency flights back to the States.

The women had strict conduct rules, which included not touching the men. But both the women and the troops were young, so there was plenty of touching—and more.

Although respect for ladies may have been lacking in Vietnam, over ten thousand women were stationed there during the war. The overwhelming majority of these women were young nurses, and an unknown number of civilian women worked for the USO, the American Friends Service Committee, Catholic Relief Services, and other humanitarian organizations. More than fifty civilian American women and eight military nurses died in Vietnam.

Except for the Vietnamese women who worked for the army, the two Red Cross workers were the only other women in our base camp. I didn't know any female nurses stationed at the field hospital in Nha Trang.

Geri Morgan, my dear friend, served as an army nurse in Vietnam. We met later while we both were stationed at a military hospital in Frankfurt, Germany,  and living in the same apartment house. Our friendship has continued for over forty-five years. She told me recently that she still has horrible flashbacks of incoming helicopters bringing in mangled and dying soldiers to be triaged at her field hospital.

For one year I lived a closeted life in a man's world. I viewed myself as a misfit among the men of the 101st and our dispensary. Absent sexual tension, I enjoyed the company of women more than macho men (and still do). I didn't cultivate a friendship with Sara, but I liked her and empathized with her pain of not being respected.

Earlier in 1966 James Brown had recorded "It's a Man's World," in which he sings: "But it wouldn't be nothing, nothing without a woman or a girl (to love)."

I would prove him wrong.

# TRAN

***11 December 1966***

*For a change of pace my friend Ken Cohen, 101st Airborne PX (Post Exchange) officer arranged dates for Rip Kirby, the club officer, himself, and me with three Vietnamese girls, who work at his PX. After chapel, I returned to meet Ken and load up a box of soft drinks into the jeep and head for Phan Rang. We checked with the MPs to verify that the road to the beach was cleared this morning and free of mines.*

*My date was Tran, a 20-year-old girl with porcelain skin and short, black shiny hair parted on the side. She moved from Nha Trang seven months ago and began working as a cashier in the PX. Her mother dislikes Americans and disapproves of Tran's association with us. Her brother, who is a 1st Lieutenant in the South Vietnamese Army, has an Army friend who wants to marry Tran, but she has no interest in him. Tran's older sister, who is 24, is a student in Tokyo. She showed me photos of her home and family, which suggest that she comes from a middle-class, or upper-middle-class, family.*

*Tran was dressed in traditional pale-blue silk ao dai with white silk pants, which is beautiful but not suitable beach wear. She told me that her mother disapproves of her wearing western clothes.*

*Lan, who was Ken's date, wore tight black slacks and a white blouse. She tied her long black silky hair into two ponytails—a very attractive girl.*

*Tran seems very shy or pretends to be. Although she finally consented, she made a big scene about me taking photos of her. She said she was afraid her mother would see the photos of her with an American. A highly unlikely scenario.*

*I didn't go swimming because it was cool and overcast. It was an enjoyable day, and I would like to go to the beach again with Tran.*

***One week later:***
*This afternoon Ken and I returned to the beach with Tran and Lan. For transportation we rented a truck owned by the Vietnamese laundry, which is located adjacent to the PX. We only paid 200 piasters for the truck and driver. Again Tran dressed in silk, traditional ao dai. Since the weather was perfect, I went swimming in the sea.*

*Later as I sat on the powdery, white sand under a pine tree, I asked Tran about her family. She told me that her mother is a devout Buddhist, but she has given Tran permission to follow the religion of her choice. Tran invited me to accompany her to visit her mother in Nha Trang the next time she goes. This makes no sense because a week ago she told me her mother didn't approve of her dating Americans.*

*Tran asked me naïve questions. "Why don't I have hair under my arms like you?" I told her not to worry because if she did she would shave like American girls.*

*I don't know if she is shy or has an inferiority complex, but in her dulcet voice she asked, "Do you think I am ugly?"*

*"No—definitely not," I said.*

What was going on with me? Perhaps Tran intrigued me because I had never dated a Vietnamese woman. Ken was my friend, and when he asked me to double date with him, "yes" was the normal response. It was important to me to pass as straight to my fellow soldiers. While trying to suppress my homosexual nature, I was hoping to date and fall in love with any woman. I was still trying to prove to myself that I could be attracted to women, and I had not accepted the fact that I was gay. By prayer and sheer willpower, I was trying to transfer my desire for men to women.

Since I was a teenager, I had been conflicted about my attraction to boys and later to men, while I continued to assiduously date girls. During the late 1950s and early '60s, society expected a good Christian young man like me to have a girlfriend. And I complied. While in high school, Sandra was my girlfriend, but Buddy Deal was my buddy. I didn't have a name for my feelings, but at school I wanted to be with Buddy as much as possible. We didn't date, but I did have a sleepover at his house. (Not to worry, his dog slept between us.) Going "all the way" with either Sandra or Buddy was a sin. And I didn't. (Two years after graduating from high school, Sandra asked me to sing at her wedding. Ironically, I sang "Wither Thou Goest I Will Go.")

My church taught me that sex outside of marriage was a sin. When I was sixteen years old, our church pastor led a sex education class for teenagers—a very progressive concept for the late 1950s in the rural South. I don't remember any mention of homosexuality in those classes, but I do remember the statement about masturbation being wrong. After all, the Bible states in Genesis 38: "But Onan knew that the offspring would not be his. So whenever he went in to his brother's wife he would waste the semen on the ground, so as not to give offspring to his brother. And what he did was wicked in the sight of the Lord, and he put him to death also." But the fear of death did not prevent me from onanism—or from having sexual thoughts about men.

I continued to date women. In optometry school, I dated Ruthie Weber for three years. I met Ruthie at church and eventually brought her home to meet my parents, but I was never physically attracted to or in love with her. I welcomed graduation and leaving Chicago to escape from any commitment beyond girlfriend.

I met Neva while attending the Larchmont Church of God (a thirty-minute drive from Fort Knox) and dated for about a year until I left for Vietnam. At a safe distance of nine thousand miles, I maintained the relationship via letters with the unrealistic goal of marrying her. After returning to the States, I drove from Fayetteville, North Carolina, to Louisville to spend the weekend with her. She was pretty and fun to be with, but it was not meant to be.

Prior to Neva, I dated Mary Ann from the same Louisville Church of God. Mary Ann's husband had drowned in a boating accident, and she had a five-year-old son. Mother expressed concern about my possible marriage to Mary Ann with her ready-made family. Not to worry. We broke up after an unpleasant weekend trip together at Anderson Camp Meeting (a national, annual gathering that formed in the late 1800s as a way for Church of God members to hear preachers and musicians and share their faith). In retrospect, I was cold and distant, and she expected more. I couldn't handle the reality of commitment and eventual marriage, not with Mary Ann, or any other woman.

How would my life have turned out without the year in Vietnam? I would probably have returned to Hickory, North Carolina, set up an optometry practice, married, and had children. Eventually I would have caused my wife and family pain and heartache because I could not have denied the core of my being. For all the misery and destruction brought on by our war in Vietnam, I am grateful for the year there, in which I began questioning, reflecting, and eventually accepting my true self.

But it shouldn't have taken a war.

# BIG GUN

***15 December 1966***

*I was ready for bed when Jim Mahoney came into the tent and said, "Let's go watch them shoot tonight." The sky was filled with stars on this clear, hot night as Jim drove the jeep to the 27th Artillery camp. The only sound—other than the noise of our jeep's engine—was crickets. The unpaved road was rough and seemed to lead to nowhere as we headed toward the camp's perimeter. With only the moon and stars lighting our way, we had to drive with our headlights off, making it difficult to find the small camp. Finally, we saw a group of men, and a soldier took us to the big gun.*

*Right on schedule at 2100 hours, the 105mm Howitzer gun belched out the twirling shells. Soldiers in the 27th Artillery receive field telephone instructions and seconds later begin firing their gun, which has a range of five to seven miles—quite a weapon. Most nights they use it for harassment fire, but also they use it for real, identified targets. The soldiers fire two to four projectiles at intervals of 10 minutes until midnight and 15-minute intervals until 0300. In the morning the Republic of Korea (ROK) forces go out to see if they have hit any VC. Sometimes they do.*

*Soldiers rotate on a 12-to-12-hour shift so some of them are always trying to sleep. I have no idea how anyone can sleep this close to the gun , because the deafening noise sometimes wakes me up in my tent, which is over a mile away. When I am awakened, I remain very still and listen again to make sure the shells are not incoming.*

*We thanked the artillery soldiers and went home. I had a terrific headache and my ears will never be the same.*

I quickly learned to never call a military pistol or rifle a "gun." The rugged Howitzer is the army's definition of a gun—a seventeen-foot barrel mounted on a frame, which was supported by two rubber tires for towing. The Airborne Infantry unit could also drop the Howitzer by parachute.

As I recall, one soldier sighted the target while two other soldiers alternated loading and removing the shell casings from the gun. Another soldier manned the telephone receiving fire orders and calibrating the coordinates.

Boys like to play with big guns, right? I didn't. Although I qualified with the .45 caliber handgun and with the M14 and M16 rifles, I never felt comfortable firing a weapon. My brothers loved to go hunting with their rifles with my Daddy or Uncle George and his beagles, but from an early age I was never interested in hunting with boys. I preferred to stay in the house with Mother and bake cookies. I knew I was different from other boys and tried to blend in, to get by, and to not be called out. I was doing the same thing in Vietnam.

# FINDING THE FECES

***22 December 22 1966***

*Tonight I met 1st Lt. Weismann wandering around our dispensary area. Since he is leaving the base camp early tomorrow morning, he wanted a test for syphilis—tonight. He insisted. Since there were no lab techs around, I drew his blood. While talking to him, I determined he was an OCS (Officer Candidate School) graduate. He was crude, uneducated and couldn't complete a sentence without including "motherfuck." He was an enlisted man for four years before OCS school.*

*I was shocked to learn that Weismann makes twice my pay, in part because of extra pay for TDY (temporary duty assignment). Weismann walked into an army office, obtained a manual on how to use the Personnel Detector and received TDY orders to evaluate its efficiency in the field.*

*The Personnel Detector, a.k.a. the "People Sniffer," was developed by General Electric under an $8 million* contract with the military. The 25-pound machine, which is carried on the soldier's back, is designed to take air samples through a hose, which is also connected to a soldier's rifle. Using beeping sounds*

* $8 million adjusted for inflation is about $175 million in today's dollars.

*received via earphones the instrument warns soldiers of the enemy's presence when ammonia fumes given off by the body combine with other chemicals. The problem with the instrument is that not only does it register the ammonia given off by human sweat, but also ammonia from body waste materials from humans, so the men in the field don't know whether the warning is triggered by a real live enemy soldier or by feces. I call it an expensive feces detector.*

*I question the reliability of the data, which is collected by an untrained lieutenant, who then trains carriers. My guess is that the reason for this data collection mission is that someone in Washington, who believed that $8 million was a high price for a feces detector and demanded data to justify its usefulness.*

Opinions about the reliability and value of the personnel detector varied among soldiers and military leaders. According to an After Action Report by the 101st Airborne Division Commanding General Matheson, from September to December 1967 the personnel detector was effective in their search-and-destroy missions in areas of heavy vegetation, where visual reconnaissance was ineffective. (The time period cited was one year after Lt. Weismann became the project officer.) The people sniffer evolved into the airborne personnel detector, which was mounted on helicopters. Flying just above trees enabled the collection and analysis of air samples, which supposedly reduced the problem of detecting soldier or animal feces.

Two years later at Fort Bragg, North Carolina, I tested new military equipment and collected data. Unlike Lt. Weismann, I wasn't paid extra, but it was an excrement-free project. Since the military rarely issued contact lenses at the time, I was assigned a test project to determine the best device to help airborne soldiers keep their spectacles on their faces when they jumped out of planes. After landing in enemy territory, you must see to carry out the mission.

First, I accompanied soldiers to the training jump towers and fitted them with three different types of straps to their spectacles. I soon discovered that jump towers were not high enough to adequately test the straps, which meant that I needed to assure they were wearing the straps properly and to test the effectiveness of the product after jumping from a plane. That is why I found myself, on a Saturday morning, surrounded by two-dozen paratroopers from the 82nd Airborne preparing to jump from a perfectly good plane.

As they hitched up their parachute straps to the main line, I got a spirited sense of the adrenaline rush troops have when preparing to jump. The jumpmaster shouted encouragement and the paratroopers responded with equally loud enthusiasm as they moved body-to-body toward the open door. They were so pumped up that I was afraid that the men might try to take me with them on the jump. That was a problem. I had no training and no parachute. I made a run for the front of the plane away from the open door and luckily I was not pushed out of the plane.

I recall back in Vietnam a paratrooper told me that jumping from an airplane gave him a stupendous rush, which was second only to having an orgasm with a woman. I can't vouch for it, but observing the unrestrained excitement of the 82nd paratroopers, I can believe it.

Mother, Daddy and me at Fort Lewis, circa 1945. I returned to Fort Lewis 21 years later as a soldier.

Boy with goats on Highway 1.

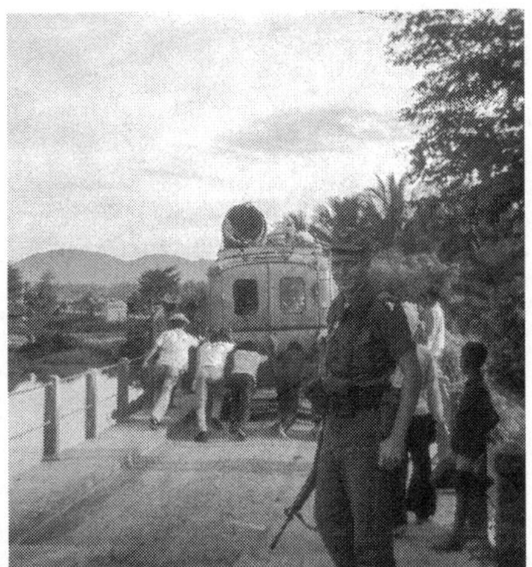

101st soldier stands guard as bus obstructs Highway 1.

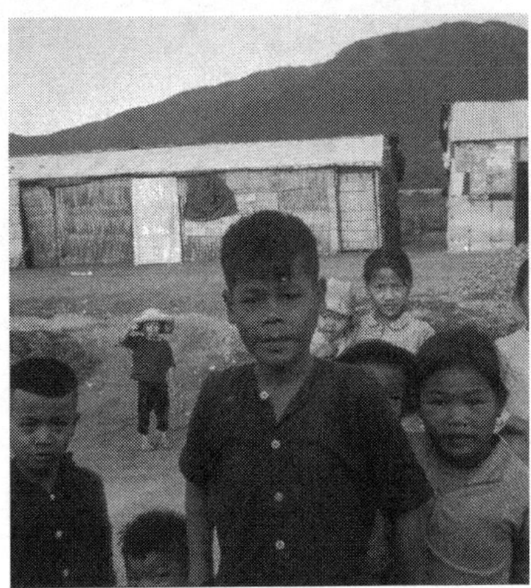

Children in hamlet near Phan Rang.

A dentist at the Sunday market in Phan Rang.

Women selling peppers in market.

Pedicabs and pedestrians at the Esso station.

Ahmet in Istanbul.

Tran.

Patients line up for eye exams at my clinic.

Sister Marie gets an eye exam.

Nancy Sinatra and USO show.

The "Strip" of bars and prostitutes.

Boarding Pan Am to Hong Kong with Peter Ricca.

Peter Ricca in Tiger Gardens.

Posing in Army skivvies in front of the Hex.

Lying in my bed of portulaca flowers wearing peasant pajamas.

Aura at beach near Bangkok.

Karlheinz and Jirina.

Rachael and me in Swiss Alps.

Sharon in Frankfurt, Germany.

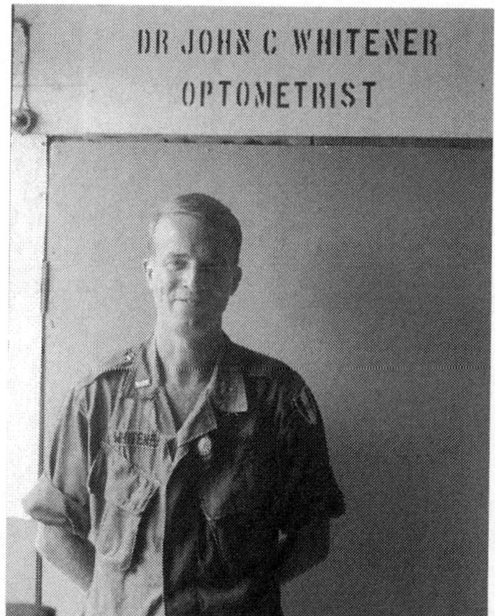


At my clinic, 1967.

In my apartment, while stationed in Frankfurt, Germany, 1970.

In my apartment at Fort Sill, 1973, one month before resigning my commission.

# BILLY GRAHAM

***23 December 1966***

*A few days ago evangelist Billy Graham, accompanied by George Beverly Shea, Cliff Barrows, and Ted Smith, arrived in Vietnam for a 10-day tour. The service held in Saigon was heavily guarded; however, when I saw him in Cam Ranh Bay, there were only a few unarmed MPs in the crowd. About 400 people were at the event, compared to 15,000 who attended the recent Bob Hope show.*

*We sang Christmas carols as Ted Smith played the piano. Mr. Shea sang "Go Tell It on the Mountain," "He's Got the Whole World in His Hands," "Roll Jordon," and a Christmas version of "How Great Thou Art." Mr. Graham quoted the famous verse from John 3:16: "For God so loved the world..." He posed questions: Why was there war in Vietnam if God loves the world? Why do we have death and destruction from a loving God?*

*He posed questions; he didn't give me the answers.*

Although I read in my journal that I attended Billy Graham's event in Vietnam, I have no recollection. Why did I suppress this memory? Was it because he didn't answer the important questions he posed? Did he stir up feelings of guilt and shame as he called us to come to Jesus to be forgiven of our sins? Probably.

This was not the first time I had been to a Billy Graham event. As a teenager, a busload of people from our church traveled to the coliseum in Charlotte, North Carolina, to see him. His message was "we are all sinners," but God will forgive us, if we repent. He continues today to include homosexuals as sinners who must repent.

Reverend Billy Graham interacted with eleven U.S. presidents of both parties, but I remain disturbed by presidential tapes from a 1972 Oval Office conversation between Nixon and Graham. The dialogue indicated that Graham shared Nixon's anti-Semitic views that Jews controlled the media. After the tapes were made public, Graham stated: "Although I have no memory of the occasion I deeply regret comments I apparently made in an Oval Office conversation with President Nixon."

Living in Asheville, I frequently read about Billy Graham and his son Franklin in the *Asheville Citizen-Times*, which covers any news about Graham—our local celebrity. Frequently, the news is about his failing health and hospitalizations.

But in 2012, I was shocked when Billy Graham paid for a full-page ad in the *Asheville Citizen-Times* to ask voters to approve an amendment to the state constitution banning same-sex marriage—a highly charged political issue.

Based on interviews I have read with his son Franklin, I believe that Franklin, not his father, was behind the anti-gay marriage newspaper ad. I am disappointed that the Graham organization has become involved in political issues, which tarnishes the name and career of Billy Graham. Franklin Graham is now the CEO of the Billy Graham Evangelistic Association, which is composed of several organizations operating around the world. He is handsomely paid for his charity work, reportedly earning $880,000 in 2014.

In the March 2014 issue of *Decision*, Franklin praised Russian President Vladimir Putin for signing a bill that fines adults in Russia who "promote propaganda of nontraditional sexual relations to minors." He went on to say that the Russian legislation protected children and that Putin's record was better than Obama's "shameful" embrace of gay rights. "Of course, gays and lesbians cannot have children," he said. "They can recruit." I am amazed at Franklin's ignorance and his prejudice.

Franklin is not alone in his abhorrence of gays and lesbians. Putin's anti-gay law has resulted in numerous beatings of gay men on the street, on subways and in nightclubs. Throughout history, and notably in Nazi Germany, first comes the anti-gay rhetoric, then demeaning laws and violence. In 2015, Republican lawmakers introduced more than eighty-five anti-gay bills in twenty-eight state legislatures.

Franklin is failing to learn a valuable lesson from his father. In his 1997 autobiography, *Just As I Am*, Billy Graham wrote, "If I had to do it over again, I would avoid any semblance of involvement in partisan politics."

In spite of Billy Graham's past, in 2015, the North Carolina General Assembly passed legislation honoring him with a statue to be placed in our nation's capitol. Since each state is permitted to display only two bronze statues to honor notable persons in their history, North Carolina legislators must remove one, which will be Charles Brantley Aycock. Aycock's record as governor was promoting increased teacher's salaries and establishing fair election machinery. While arguing that the Negro should not be permitted to vote, he also supported a law to prevent lynching. Now his white supremacy views have been revealed.

Aycock's statute is being removed because of his racist views, and replaced by Graham, who has expressed anti-gay and anti-Semitic views. Two wrongs don't make a right, right? I am appalled.

Billy Graham always used his Bible while preaching in his crusades, and took the words of the book seriously, if not literally. I'm not sure if he preached from Exodus 20: "You shall have no other gods before me. You shall not make for yourself a carved image, or any likeness of anything that is in heaven above, or that is in the earth beneath, or that is in the water under the earth."

While he may not have preached against "carved images," I know he used other scriptures to condemn people like me. I clearly remember his hell-fire TV sermons from my youth. Too bad I can't remember any of his sermons about Jesus' love and acceptance of all God's children—even me.

# CHRISTMAS EVE WITH THE STRIPPER

***24 December 1966***

*'Twas the night before Christmas*
*And anyone could see,*
*Not a creature was sober*
*Except Ron, Smitty, Dave and me.*

*On a busy, enjoyable, routine Saturday morning, I examined seven patients. But things began to go wrong in the afternoon when our softball game was called off due to a misunderstanding. While our men were out in the field warming up, Company A called to confirm the game. Unfortunately, Spec. 5 Gregory answered the dispensary's phone and told them the game was cancelled. Gregory strikes out again.*

*In the afternoon, with sweat running down our faces and flies buzzing around our heads, Sgt. Hall and I decorated a green, four-foot artificial tree using three sets of miniature blinking lights and three dozen multicolored balls. When we finished, it resembled a Special Services' honest-to-goodness artificial Christmas tree. Although I didn't place them under the Christmas tree, I have received a few Christmas presents of cookies and goodies from family and friends.*

*Words fail me as I try to describe the vulgarity, filth, and crudeness of this Christmas Eve. The men in our unit began drinking early today and haven't let up. The enlisted men built a bar several weeks ago in one of their sleeping tents, and this afternoon it is full of drunks. About an hour after we had eaten grilled steaks, our ambulance pulled up to the dispensary and unloaded six Vietnamese prostitutes from the Strip. The evening turned into a mass orgy, but it was all in the holiday spirit—the girls were giving their gifts freely.*

*I escaped the drunken orgy by walking to the 101st Airborne's outdoor staged Christmas Eve show, which began with a Vietnamese band attempting to play their version of American music. The music was so bad that the audience of several hundred drunken GIs began throwing beer cans at the band. At one point several men jumped onstage, grabbed the guitars and drums from the band, and began playing. The military police restored order and the Vietnamese band resumed playing their rotten renditions of "Dixie" and "Jingle Bells."*

*Thirty minutes into their bad music, an unattractive blonde, Mira, bounced onto the stage. She wore a tight, glittering, unbecoming red dress with a white, mock fur cape. As she began peeling off her clothes, it became apparent that she was not Mrs. Santa Claus. I wanted to vomit. Although this was not a USO-sanctioned holiday show (a sergeant had discovered her in Nha Trang), Mira fully displayed the spirit of the season by sharing the gift of her voluptuous body with the fighting men of 101st Airborne.*

*I will never forget this Christmas Eve surrounded by hundreds of drunken men, a strip act and an orgy.*

My visceral response to Mira seems extreme, but my parents and church inculcated in me high moral values and the proper role of women: virtuous women didn't expose their bodies in public. But perhaps more importantly: I wasn't interested.

Also, the Vietnamese prostitutes prompted memories of dallying with two women in Malaysia. The Apostle Paul, a bachelor like myself, warned Christians: "Make not provision for the flesh to gratify its desires." I didn't make provision that Christmas Eve, but I was guilt-ridden about previous provisions.

I think I was envious of the men who were making provision for sex with women, and I couldn't. Nor could I have sex with men. Fortunately for all, I was not attracted to any men in my unit.

On that Christmas Eve, I didn't have a church, pastor, or friend to turn to for refuge. There was not a candlelight chapel service or carols to be heard. I missed my church, family, and everything that was familiar.

Spiritually, I was running on empty. This had been the worst Christmas Eve of my life.

# CELEBRATING CHRISTMAS

***25 December 1966***

*Surrounded by the noise from our inebriated troops, I got very little sleep last night. Although I slept later than usual this morning, I dressed, shaved, and still arrived on time for the 0900 chapel service. Our new chaplain's boring, long, sanitized sermon was titled "The Three Dimensions of Christmas"—In reach, Up reach and Out reach. I failed to connect the relevance of the sermon's message to my life. Certainly it was not inspirational.*

*I returned to our camp where Smitty asked me to ride with him in the truck into the village to pick up our dispensary's Vietnamese workers—Linh, Minh, Mia, and Jack, as well as Tran for our Christmas Day celebration. We drove around the village for an hour finding their houses. When we returned to camp, it was lunchtime, and the workers ate lunch with the enlisted men. The officers and enlisted men's mess featured the same menu—traditional baked turkey with all the trimmings, served on a metal tray. The mess tent was gaily decorated with a Christmas tree.*

*I spent the afternoon with Tran and realized that she is very immature. At 1630 we took the Vietnamese workers home. Christmas Day was becoming mostly depressing.*

*I heard there was a Christmas show tonight, which I hoped*

*would cheer me up. After arriving at the staging area, I realized it was another non-sanctioned strip show. The feature was Babette Blake from India and more recently from London, but currently operating out of Saigon. She made the audience wait for almost an hour, which increased the anticipation—and beer drinking.*

*Unlike the fake blonde from last night, Babette put on a real show with taped Indian music. Under the glow of red-hot and orange spotlights, she slowly, but surely, ground out a simulation of every possible sex position I could imagine in front of hundreds of screaming, sex-starved GIs. What a morale booster! A perfect Christmas show. Not.*

*Later outside my tent I watched a Christmas display of lights. Red tracers and green flares fired from the Replacement Company's training group illuminated the night. Jet engines from the Phan Rang Air Base—not Christmas carols sung by a choir—provided a deafening roar for the light show. My mind was flooded with thoughts and memories of other Christmas Days with my family.*

*"Peace on earth" feels like a meaningless phrase .*

So where do I start? On some level of consciousness, I was trying to develop a relationship with Tran. The explicit events are muddled for that afternoon so many Christmases ago. I do remember that we had tea in my tent and talked. We did not exchange gifts.

Maybe it was the sight of a Christmas strip show mixed with the sound of Indian music and the howling of hundreds of drunken soldiers that made me sad. While I berated soldiers for their sexual exploits and vulgar sexual bantering, I recall that Jesus said, "He who is without sin let him cast the first stone." I was not without sin.

Whatever it was, the celebration of Christmas in Vietnam had nothing to do with Jesus, with faith, or even with goodwill toward others. It was a demonstration of the worst in human nature rather than the best.

And I learned an important lesson about myself that day. I discovered that being true to myself and my faith—at least on Christmas Day—was more important than fitting in.

# FINISHED

***26 December 26 1966***

*For several mornings Tran has stopped by to visit me while I am at work in the clinic. These unannounced visits really bug me. This morning I told her that she was a nice, pretty young lady, but I didn't want to continue dating her.*

*"Are the photos you took of me at the beach mine?" she asked.*

*"Yes."*

*She reached into her purse and pulled out five photos. Calmly she tore four of the five photos into small pieces. After she discovered that she had saved the wrong photo, she tore it into pieces, as well. I was flummoxed. Perhaps she felt bad about her actions because she then offered me one of her own studio photographs. I accepted it and she signed it "Tran."*

*She told me that she realized her big mistake in coming to visit me at my office. She was very upset and would not be able to work at the PX today. I told her she couldn't go home without telling Lt. Cohen, her boss. She wrote a note to him stating she was ill and asked me to give him the note.*

*What a silly mess. Tran and I are finished.*

My whirlwind two weeks of dating Tran ended as quickly as it began. From that relationship I have a photograph and peasant pajamas, which Tran sewed for me. (The material was part of a cache of Viet Cong spoils taken by 101st soldiers.)

Looking back on my dating patterns in my teens and twenties, I always found a reason to break up with my girlfriends. While it was inappropriate for Tran to visit me during office hours, I could have told her to stop the office visits, and our dating could have continued. We had two dates at the beach and several teatime visits in my tent. Yes, tea in my small tent, which was just big enough for two cots and two footlockers.

I didn't record it in my journal, but I remember at least one teatime visit when I touched her. Or was it a kiss? I don't think that I tried to kiss her because I didn't like to kiss girls. It was unnatural for me. I can't be sure, but perhaps I attempted to touch Tran's breast to convince myself I was normal. If so, it didn't work. There was no passion. No sparks. The whole scene seems to play out through a colored gel filter creating unnatural effects. I was playing an actor in a naughty French farce, in a tent in Vietnam. Or maybe a peccant actor impersonating a straight soldier.

I do remember her saying, "No," and I ceased all advances—whatever they may have been. Perhaps I remember the warning from the Apostle Paul to the Corinthians: It is good for a man to not touch a woman.

Back in the seventh grade, a favorite party game was spin the bottle, and my first kiss was with Janelda (or was it Jackie?). I reluctantly participated. When I began dating girls, I dreaded the required perfunctory kiss at the end of the evening. But I enjoyed kissing Buddy Deal, beginning in the eighth grade. In broad daylight, we kissed (more than on one occasion) while riding in the school bus. Our justification was to freak out (and we did) an older girl, who sat in front of us and expressed disgust at our kissing. Looking back, I am amazed that the tough boys didn't pulverize me. It was 1955 (think: Eisenhower administration and TV's *Father Knows Best*) and the place was rural North Carolina.

I prayed for God to change me as I tried to suppress my

homosexual feelings. When I had learned from church teachings that masturbation was a sin, I prayed to stop and relapsed...and relapsed.

In neither case were my prayers answered.

Perhaps I should have been praying the prayer of Augustine: "Lord, make me pure…but not yet."

# NEW YEAR

***1 January 1967***

*I took communion in chapel on this first Sunday, first day of the year. With all my doubts and confusion about my faith, I asked God to help my unbelief.*

*Today was quiet compared to last night. Several drunks staggered into the dispensary with minor abrasions, including one young sergeant who was high on marijuana. Many of the enlisted men in the unit were blitzed, and the sound of barfing interrupted the music from the "Grand Ole Opry"—the only English-speaking station I could pick up.*

*At 1400, Lt. Col.. Abood held a New Year's Day reception at the officers' club. I stayed a short time and left with Lt. Lane McNitt to see his Replacement Company's collection of snakes, monkeys and parrots. The collection was housed in cages built of wood, glass and cement. McNitt pointed out pit vipers, a 12-foot boa constrictor and water snakes. All the snakes are used for instructional purposes, to acquaint newly arrived troops with the snakes of the area.*

*Tonight I went to the 62nd Engineer's chapel to hear the Phan Rang Orphanage Choir. The children ranged in ages from 10-14 and were directed by their Vietnamese pastor, who also played the organ. The children sang in English, "All Hail the Power of Jesus' Name," "How Great Thou Art," and "Hallelujah"; however, most hymns were sung in Vietnamese. The Vietnamese pastor spoke a few minutes and an offering was taken to help build a Bible School for the children. A good ending to the first day of the year.*

New Year's Day is about new beginnings and resolutions. I began and ended the day in chapel asking for a new beginning, a cleansing of my soul. Although I didn't find any answers for reconciling my sexual orientation with God, I continued to attend chapel services throughout my tour in Vietnam.

Even though I was spiritually adrift, I persevered. I read my Bible, and I prayed. Still questioning, yet still hoping for answers.

# POT

***14 January 1967***

*Today I was one of five members of a Special Court-Martial, which took place in Cam Ranh Bay. Our medical battalion headquarters ordered Ron Walker to be the defense counsel and me to be a member of the three-person panel.*

*The defendants were two soldiers who were accused of possession of marijuana. Neither soldier was accused of dealing or selling. The evidence confiscated by the military police was sent for testing to a military lab in Japan; however, a lab representative was not present for the trial. The prosecution had only a photostat copy of a telegram from the lab with no official verification of the test results. As the appointed defense counsel, Walker immediately disqualified the admittance of this undocumented evidence. The prosecution then requested an indefinite recess in order to summon a lab man as an expert witness.*

*The whole process lasted less than an hour. I was impressed by the performance of Walker and the President of the Court, Maj. O'Kelly, the Executive Officer of our medical battalion. They talked the military lingo and seemed confident in their actions.*

*Walker was not a lawyer, but a special court-martial did not* *require a military lawyer.* Given the rapid buildup of troops during this time period, there were not enough military attorneys, due to the large number of cases.*

*The consequences of a conviction for possession of even a small amount of marijuana was up to twelve months of confinement, three months of hard labor without confinement, forfeiture of two-thirds pay per month for up to one year, reduction in pay grade, and a bad conduct discharge.*

*According to the U.S. Army Center of Military History, 1,688 persons were arrested for use of marijuana in 1967. Marijuana cigarettes were cheap and easily accessed in urban areas compared to the boonies, where I was stationed. Although I have no memory of anyone in our dispensary smoking marijuana, I later discovered that soldiers using non-medical drugs became a significant problem for the military during this time period in Vietnam. First pot, then heroin.*

*While soldiers caught using marijuana were court-martialed, alcoholism was certainly ignored or largely tolerated by the military. My tent mate drank every night and he frequently passed out in his office or acted up in the officers' club. No repercussions. Because of my teetotaler religious beliefs, I never fit into the beer drinking or drug crowd.*

Who was I to sit on a court-martial board and judge another soldier who violated the Uniform Code of Military Justice? Article 125 of the UCMJ also prohibited sodomy, which it defined as "unnatural carnal copulation." The maximum penalty for consensual sodomy under Article 125 was five years of hard labor, forfeiture of pay, and a dishonorable discharge.

If convicted under UCMJ, I would be judged less harshly for possessing pot than having consensual sex with a man. Later in my career, I ignored the penalties of the UCMJ on both counts.

---

*Subsequently, the practice of using non-legal counsel has been challenged in court for failing the requirements of the Sixth Amendment right to counsel and the Fifth Amendment's due process.

# BIRTHDAY AT THE CLUB

***21 January 1967***

For *over a year, the 1st Brigade of the 101st Airborne Division has been fighting in the rice paddies and jungles of the Central Highlands. This week soldiers packed all their gear, cleared and traveled 400 miles by jeep and truck to their base camp here at Phan Rang. A big sign stretched across the road at the entrance read: "The Can Do Battalion Welcomes the Always First Brigade." The welcome was short-lived as soldiers were assigned details including painting buildings and cutting weeds. The remaining soldiers began operations into the surrounding countryside.*

*This morning the sky was filled with 20 choppers providing support to the troops. I can see the smoke rising from the distant mountains where jet fighters are dropping bombs. The 101st is trying to push an estimated four battalions of VC from Phan Rang south and east into the sea. If they go to the sea, the marines are waiting for them. If the VC go south, they will be met by troops moving north from Saigon. So we are told.*

*With the return of the entire brigade, I am swamped with patients. Today my workload reached an all-time high of 30 patients. I also received 143 pairs of spectacles from the Optical Lab in Nha Trang.*

*Tonight the 1st Brigade hosted a goodbye party for General Willard Pearson, who completed his tour and is returning to the States. The Red Cross Recreation Center was packed with officers enjoying free booze and a buffet.*

*Today is my 25th birthday.*

I don't know why, but I don't recall telling anyone that it was my birthday. Perhaps I felt there was nothing to celebrate at this point in my life. Especially in the officer's club, which on other nights had hosted similar farewell parties with steaks and prostitutes—meat and flesh. I was uncomfortable watching men in their thirties and forties hustle eighteen-year-old Vietnamese girls.

Throughout my military career, I never felt at ease in officers' clubs. I think partly because I didn't drink alcohol, which was the heart of social interaction. Also, I could never adapt the larger-than-life swagger of the good old boys. Since I wanted to be promoted, I did what was expected of me, including attending farewell and promotion parties. While I raised my glass of Coke in a series of toasts, at the same time I resented the military's edict that officers attend all social functions.

The 101st Club was no different. While other men drank, told jokes and laughed, I was always on guard that I would say something to cause my fellow soldiers to suspect my sexual orientation. I worked to make sure that I looked and acted (thanks to Little Theater experience) like the other officers, but I was an outsider, an observer.

# MAKING RIPPLES IN THE POND

***27 January 1967***

*Today I received a phone call from the S4 (supply office) of the 61st Medical Battalion in Cam Ranh accusing me of writing lies to the Surgeon General's office at the Pentagon and creating an unfavorable impression of our battalion. Lt. Burchard was very angry and used crude language that was unbecoming to an officer. I terminated the conversation. Tomorrow I leave for Cam Ranh to sit on a court-martial board and will be confronted by the battalion commanding officer for my actions.*

*I wrote the letter to Ltc. Billy Greene, the Army Chief Optometrist in the Surgeon General's office. I described to him how I had sat idle until I scrounged enough equipment to begin work.*

*What infuriated the 61st Battalion was my statement that all my equipment was obtained through my own efforts without the assistance of my brigade or 32nd Medical Supply. The closing statement was the clincher: "My biggest gripe is that neither the 61st Medical Battalion nor the 32nd Medical Depot has assisted me in any way."*

*After nearly five months in Vietnam and still without my original equipment, I believed that I was justified in stating that I had received no assistance in obtaining my equipment. According to Maj. O'Kelly, Executive Officer, and Ltc. Irvin, Commanding Officer for the Medical Battalion, I lied. They had documented proof that they had sent requests to locate the equipment. "After all," emphasized O'Kelly, "it is not our job to locate your equipment. It is the responsibility of the transportation corps."*

*Ltc. Greene placed my letter into official channels at the Pentagon that went to Saigon's MACV Surgeon General with a request for a complete investigation of the charges made. The letter was then read to a joint meeting of medical supply officers in Saigon, causing "undue embarrassment" to the 61st Battalion staff. I was chastised. Maj. O'Kelly was furious and told me the case was not closed.*

*My policy in the military has always been to not call attention to myself—don't make ripples in the pond. The letter, my one deviation from this policy, has created giant waves.*

***One week later:***
*Maj. O'Kelly ordered me and my dispensary commanding officer and executive officer to his headquarters in Cam Ranh. He ranted and raved for an hour while Ltc. Irvin remained calm and suggested that I write a letter of apology. The reprisal I fear is that O'Kelly will hold up my promotion to captain in April. If I'm not promoted on time, I'm prepared to write my congressman in protest and cast an even larger stone into the pond.*

Since Vietnam was the first war in which optometrists served in dispensaries and hospitals, I wrote the letter to Lt. Col. Greene to inform him what was going on in the field. I had no idea that he would forward the letter on to the military command headquarters in Saigon. I don't regret writing the letter, but I should have used personal stationery instead of army letterhead.

A life lesson learned: Never jump the official chain of command without consequences.

# TET

***3 February 1967***

*When I saw fire break out in the PX beer and soda storage lot next door, my first thought was that we were under attack. Exploding soda cans flew through the air until our dispensary corpsmen used water from our storage cans to put out the fire. Later in the day the PX officer had a one-cent sale of hot Dr Pepper and other damaged soda cans. The remainder of the day was quiet, but that would change—after all, it was the Tet holiday. Attacks were expected.*

***4 February 1967***

*At 0130 I was awakened by someone screaming, "Medic, we've got a wounded man here!" The military police's house in downtown Phan Rang was blown up by VC. The MP was awakened by an explosion and small-arms fire, jumped out of bed and drove himself to our dispensary. After working on him for more than an hour, the docs determined that his burns and abrasions were severe enough to helivac him to the 8th Field Hospital in Nha Trang.*

*Seventeen men lived in the two-story house that was attacked; however, four were in Nha Trang, several on patrol, and two were shacking up with women in the village. The house was completely destroyed. The cheap cement used in construction scattered into multiple missiles by the blast, causing contusions and burns for seven other MPs. The MP on guard duty shot and killed one VC.*

*The thump-thump-thump from chopper blades and light from flares filled the night sky, making it impossible to sleep.*

***9 February 1967***

*Tet had its origins in the ancient concept of the cycle of the four seasons. The farmers plant seed in the spring, it grows in the summer until it matures and is harvested in the fall, and then the land lies quietly fallow in the winter. The coming of spring marked the beginning of a new cycle of life and the start of a new year. Just as trees begin budding after losing their dry and dead leaves, people are to shed their worries and forget about past mistakes. People look to the New Year with hope for prosperity and joy. I need a little Tet in my life.*

*The holiday (think New Year's Eve and Thanksgiving combined) is a joyful occasion for families getting together for a big meal and paying respect to their ancestors. The family wears new clothes and friendly greetings are exchanged, because to begin the New Year with anger or insults is to risk the consequence of bad fortune. The first visitor to cross the family's threshold will determine prosperity for the New Year.*

*Tonight Marv, Gene, Ron, Jim and I had an invitation to attend dinner in a private home in the village, but we declined due to potential danger in the area. We knew that earlier today soldiers from the 2/17th Cavalry were sent out because of suspected enemy activity around Phan Rang.*

*I wanted to attend the celebration dinner, but felt it was unwise. I hope the family I was to visit found another visitor with a positive attitude and disposition, and they have a good New Year.*

An official cease-fire was in place during Tet; however, VC activity in Phan Rang and other areas of Vietnam continued during the seven-day holiday.

One year later during Tet, Vietcong and North Vietnamese Army (NVA) troops waged a surprise, prolonged attack on major cities, numerous villages, and U.S. bases throughout South Vietnam. The attacks began in Central South Vietnam with particularly intense fighting in Hue waging more than three weeks. The NVA and VC were unsuccessful in winning significant battles but demonstrated that U.S. troops were vulnerable. Back home, the Tet Offensive shocked Americans who thought we were winning the war. Our strategy of counterinsurgency, bombing the North, and increasing troop strength had failed. We were losing the war.

Public support of the war was fading. Two months after the disastrous Tet Offensive, President Johnson announced he would not run for re-election. But the U.S. continued bombing the North for another five years. The Paris Peace Accords, in which the U.S. agreed to withdraw all forces, was signed in January 1973. Three months after the Paris Accords, I resigned my commission and left the Vietnam War experience behind. But my prolonged spiritual war continued.

# NANCY SINATRA

***10 February 1967***

*The first big-name USO show to come to Phan Rang was Nancy Sinatra. What a disappointment. The show began with a rock-and-roll group—a forgettable group, who could provide backup for any singer. The show also included an MC, who told a continuous string of gross jokes.*

*And then came Nancy wearing a red, white and blue striped miniskirt (how patriotic) and, of course, baby blue boots up to her knees. Her long blond hair blew in her face, which was covered with thick makeup and heavy eye shadow. She looked and sounded wretched, and her voice was neither dulcet nor strong. Her musical numbers, including "These Boots Are Made for Walking," were presentable when the background group drowned out her voice. Her final number was a fitting caption for the entire show—"Ain't No Big Thing."*

My, my, that was a bad review. Perhaps the sound system was to blame. In retrospect, I credit Nancy Sinatra for leaving the safety and luxury of home to entertain the troops. She was at the height of her popularity, and I don't think this stint in Vietnam was necessary to boost her career.

Nancy Sinatra's show in Phan Rang came one year after the release of her number-one hit, "These Boots Are Made for Walking," which was produced by Lee Hazelwood. I love the fantastic double bass guitar run at the beginning of the song. Unfortunately, the magic of the studio recording didn't carry through to her live performance. Maybe she was just having a bad day, or perhaps I was having a bad day.

Now I listen weekly to Nancy, who hosts Siriusly Sinatra on Sirius Radio. She tells stories about her daddy and herself and the musicians behind the recording. One of her stories reminded me that she sang the theme for the James Bond film *You Only Live Twice*, released in 1967—the same year I saw her touring Vietnam.

How was I to know that Nancy and her boots would become a gay icon of the seventies? In recent years she has also supported veterans groups at events that paid homage to those missing and lost in action in Vietnam. I look back on her show in Phan Rang and am grateful for her support.

# COURT-MARTIAL TRIAL

***11 February 1967***

*Ron Walker and I traveled to Cam Ranh to sit on a panel for another court-martial trial. Pfc. Victor was charged with illegal possession and use of marijuana and failure to obey a direct order from his supervising sergeant and commanding officer. He pled guilty to all charges.*

*According to Victor he had been under psychiatric treatment to stop smoking marijuana when he was caught. The CID* questioned him for several hours and then released him to return to work. Victor said he was very upset, because he had never been in trouble. He tried to return to his desk work, but the paper became blurred, and his eyes hurt. He asked his NCO if he could have the night off so he could see a doctor. The NCO said, "No. Return to work."*

*Victor tried to explain the circumstances, but his sergeant refused to listen. He then said, "I'm leaving because I can't see well enough to do my work." On the way out the door he passed his CO, who told him to return to work. He refused.*

---

* CID refers to the Criminal Investigation Command. It retains the "D" today as a historical reminder of the first Criminal Investigation Division formed in 1918 during World War I.

*Pfc. Victor was definitely in the wrong, but I felt sorry for him. He appeared to be a quiet, introverted, nervous kid. After the testimony was completed, I voted to give him the lightest possible sentence. The remainder of the panel members voted against my recommendation. We then voted on the next lightest sentence, which still didn't receive a majority of votes. The third lightest sentence passed which was three months of hard labor with confinement, three months forfeiture of two-thirds of base pay and reduction from Pfc. to Pvt. I don't agree that hard labor with confinement is appropriate punishment, but I was overruled.*

*What is justice?*

From the first day of basic training, soldiers are taught to obey. Article 90 of the Uniformed Code of Military Justice makes it a crime for soldiers to willfully disobey a superior commissioned officer, and Victor had disobeyed his CO's order to return to work. While I understand that following lawful orders is the foundation for military effectiveness, I have witnessed many cases of verbal abuse and unnecessary display of power by superior officers.

I believed that extenuating circumstances for Victor's conduct should have been taken into account for a lesser sentence. I don't recall his doctor testifying at the trial, and perhaps Victor invented the story about his treatment. Although I am an optometrist, I was not asked to respond to Victor's eye complaint. Marijuana can dilate the pupils, which can cause blurred vision. I should have queried the prosecutor and pointed out the possible validity of Victor's visual complaint.

Looking back, I think it was difficult for me to vote for sentencing Victor to three months of hard labor with confinement, which could have made him into a hardened criminal. Perhaps I was pushing for the lightest punishment for Victor, because I wanted to show mercy for Victor, and in turn, mercy for myself.

# RECREATION

***12 February 1967***

*Tonight at supper Margot and Sara (from the Red Cross) told about their recent adventure. They had taken several board games and quizzes to Phan Thiet to entertain the troops, but the men had other games in mind. The men had the afternoon off duty and said that they were going to the shower point or to the beach, and they could come with them. The girls chose the beach, but some of the men, who didn't get the word, didn't bring their swimming suit. The girls were given cut-off fatigues and t-shirts while the men swam nude.*

*According to one of the troopers, the beach experience was fun especially when the waves washed Margot's "big boobs" out of her shirt. God bless our Red Cross girls.*

***15 February 1967***

*Margot, the short, plump, curvaceous, blond girl, will be leaving shortly for reassignment. Rumor has it that Col. Sunday and Maj. Hobbs were making a routine check of the perimeter and found Margot making out with an enlisted Negro soldier in the grass. Red Cross recreation, indeed.*

Okay, so life could be boring without a TV, smartphone, or iPad.

There were only two women—both Red Cross workers—living in our base camp with hundreds of lascivious young men. For guys who wanted female companionship, there was little choice other than the prostitutes at the Strip.

***17 February 1967***

*Fun, drinking, diarrhea, and sensual pleasure (or a combination of all four) are available only a short walking distance from the perimeter of our base camp at the Strip. Troopers are lined up as early as 0800 at the gate waiting for the bars to open. Later in the day MPs patrol the Strip and pick up drunken soldiers and return them back to base.*

*The Strip consists of two long rows of bars, restaurants and dance halls facing each other and separated by a 75-foot-wide red dirt street, which is littered with cans, discarded food, begging children, old people, dogs, dope peddlers, and most anything else you can imagine. Today I went to see for myself and found it disgusting.*

*Standing in the doors of the bars were prostitutes wearing tight-fitting western clothes and revealing as much flesh as possible below their neck. Their faces were covered with copious amounts of powder, rouge and lipstick, which masked their real age. Soldiers strolled in the dusty street scanning their prospects at the New York, Florida, Texas, Shadows, Kinky or another bar.*

*I choose to go into the Red Dragon Bar, which was next door to the Texas. My eyes took a few minutes to adjust to the dark, red-lit interior when I saw a young girl who wore the traditional ao dai. She sat down beside me and explained that the Dragon does not offer "boom-boom" facilities in its back rooms—only drinking and talking. Okay with me. I ordered a Coke, but didn't drink it when I realized it was bottled in Vietnam.*

*I left and went to another bar, which featured a loud, lousy Vietnamese rock-and-roll band playing as girls hopped on soldiers' laps. While dogs stretched lazily in the corner, little kids rode around the bar on tricycles and another kid pulled a wagon. Three little dirty kids in ragged clothing came up to me and handed me a note: "Please give money to my hungry children as I am sick and cannot work. Please give as little as possible."*

In 1967, prostitution was illegal under Vietnamese law and yet sex for money was available in hair salons, massage parlors, bars, and brothels. In order to have some control over their troops seeking prostitutes, the military made unofficial agreements with brothels.* There were scores of prostitutes working at the Strip.

Dr. Henry Hamilton, a British volunteer doctor who lived in the village and worked in the Phan Rang civilian hospital, established a VD clinic at the Strip. Each week Dr. Hamilton and doctors from Phan Rang Airbase visited the brothels to test the women for venereal diseases. Each woman was tested monthly, which I suppose is better than no testing. If the brothel owner refused to allow testing of his prostitutes, the military could put the bar "off limits." The air force base docs also kept a book with photos of the prostitutes and the names of the bars where they worked. When airmen tested positive for VD, they were asked the name of the bar and to try to identify the prostitute. Even though our dispensary's VD clinic had more visits than any other clinic, we didn't make a public health effort to prevent the spread of disease. I don't think our dispensary docs were asked, nor do I recall them volunteering to help with the VD screening. I don't know why.

I learned that several months after I left Phan Rang, the 101st Airborne docs began supplying equipment and medicine for use in the Strip clinic. While U.S. military commanders knew that their troops contracted VD from prostitutes at the Strip, they hesitated to be associated with sanctioned, monitored prostitution.

The bars in the Strip were designated brothels or "tea bars." (The Red Dragon, where I had my Coke, was a tea bar.) A tea bar sold drinks, but the girls were not to have sex with customers. Regardless, Dr. Hamilton insisted on periodically examining all girls

---

*Since 2008, the Uniform Code of Military Justice (UCMJ), Article 134 prohibits service members from engaging in sexual intercourse for monetary gain or offering money to carry out intercourse. Maximum penalty is forfeiture of all allowance and pay, dishonorable discharge, and one year's confinement.

in both tea bars and brothels. Being concerned with prevention, he reasoned that all the girls—even the tea bar girls—were susceptible to having sex with GIs and thus spreading VD.

I went to the Strip because one of the guys in my unit insisted I go with him. I was not interested in having sex with any of the women, but I was curious to check it out. Recently, I found an out-of-focus photo of myself with my arm around the young girl in the dimly lit Red Dragon. Placing my arm around the girl was expected behavior in my role as a single, heterosexual soldier. I complied and even managed a fake smile.

# SISTER MARIE

***2 March 1967***

*Dr. Palma from the Air Force dispensary brought in two Vietnamese nuns for visual examinations this morning. A lovely Vietnamese girl, probably about age 19, interpreted. The older nun complained that her eyes hurt while reading. She had approximately 20/20 visual acuity at distance and near, and I could find no cause for her complaint or need for glasses. Perhaps her true visual problem was lost in translation.*

*Sister Marie Emmanuel was a different case. She appeared to be about 24-years old, bright and shy, and had a genuine visual problem. She entered my office wearing glasses with -3.75 diopters in each eye; however, when I used the retinoscope I discovered only -1.00 in the right eye and -.25 in the left. Her subjective responses in the exam were erratic and inconsistent. Her myopia was significantly overcorrected with her glasses.*

Sister Marie Emmanuel could have been wearing previously-used eyeglasses. It happens. Numerous well-meaning volunteer groups collect used spectacles and send them to developing countries for distribution. In addition to frequently wearing incorrect prescriptions, individuals can have diseases that remain undetected without an ocular exam. I do not support groups who send used glasses to developing countries without building a sustainable infrastructure for continuous eye care.

I examined three Vietnamese patients during my entire year in Phan Rang. One patient was the young girlfriend of a soldier. He told me, "I don't think she can see. She runs into things."

After examining her, I agreed. She was extremely myopic—needing glasses nineteen times stronger than Sister Marie's. I turned to the soldier and said, "Your girlfriend has never seen your face. Are you sure you want her to get glasses?" We both laughed, and I assured the girl that she was going to see a whole new world.

I have regrets about our war in Vietnam. I was a part of the military machine in Vietnam that killed hundreds of thousands of civilians. At least I helped two Vietnamese women.

# PRESIDENT OF THE COURT

***3 March 1967***

*I went to Cam Ranh to be on another Court-Martial Board for two cases. Pfc. Little's case was tonight and Pfc. Adams will come before the board tomorrow.*

*Pfc. Little was charged with falling asleep while on guard duty. He was found sleeping by his commanding officer. Unlike previous Court-Martial Boards in which I had participated, Little had a real lawyer for defense counsel. Immediately the lieutenant lawyer challenged Maj. O'Kelly, the President, off the Board. (The defense lawyer can remove one of the five Board members without cause.)*

*Since I was the next highest-ranking officer remaining, I became the President, or in civilian terms, the judge. I was terrified as my eyes darted to Maj. O"Kelly, who smiled. I hadn't prepared for this scenario. This is only the fourth case I've witnessed, and now I'm responsible for insuring a fair trial to the accused. My guess is that the lawyer smartly challenged Maj. O'Kelly off the Board to play upon my inexperience.*

*The young soldier had already pleaded guilty. Simple case, right?*

*So I thought. The lawyer brought in four witnesses to testify mostly on hearsay evidence that Little's quarters was the scene of partying on the nights previous to his guard duty. (Later I discovered that he hadn't bothered to interview the witnesses in advance.) It was boring to hear the same story from each soldier; however, one man who slept in the same house as Little added some vitality to the otherwise dull proceedings. The witness stalled for several seconds trying to think of another word, but he finally blurted it out. The soldier said, "I woke up in the morning after the party to find that someone had pissed in my boot." I was having difficulty figuring out how urine in a friend's boot is connected to the case of a soldier falling asleep on guard duty.*

*According to Little, an extenuating circumstance caused him to fall asleep. Under sworn testimony he stated, "I took a pill given by a friend to help me stay awake." Unknown to Little, the pill turned out to be a tranquilizer. A stupid mistake.*

*Here is a portion of the transcript of the defense lawyer making his closing argument to the court:*

> *Now I will not bore the court to tears because the facts are obvious. Pfc. Little admits that he did fall asleep, because he could no longer stay awake, on or about 0530 hours on the morning of 2 January. You have heard testimony of how for the previous two nights there was noise and chaos in Little's quarters, which prevented him from sleeping. He had been nervous and tense for some time which prevented him from sleeping so he took a pill to relax. Of course, the tranquilizer made matters worse, but he's not on trial for taking a tranquilizer.*
>
> *You also heard testimony that Little was not issued ammunition for his weapon so even if Charlie attacked, he could do nothing but perhaps call for help. May I remind the court that we're not in Phan Rang with the 101st Airborne or with the 1st Cavalry, we're in Cam Ranh Bay—that quiet, peaceful sanctuary amid a war torn country where the VC have never fired a shot. Some people say that the reason Charlie never bothers Cam Ranh is because he steals all the supplies he needs from the ships coming into*

> *the harbor. Be that as it may, Cam Ranh is a safe haven and that is where Little was on guard duty, and there is where he fell asleep the last 30 minutes of his duty—not out in the boonies where life and death are imminent.*
>
> *May I suggest to the court—and I realize this is a bold suggestion—that the maximum sentence be a fine of $20 for three months, because the pocketbook is going to be a reminder of his punishment each month when he draws $20 less than usual.*
>
> *You have heard statements from his former platoon leader, his present platoon leader and his CO that Pfc. Little is neither the best nor worst soldier in his platoon. He is an average soldier. Also you heard testimony that he is the type person that would learn his lesson without maximum punishment. Again, may I suggest a maximum punishment of $20 fine for three months.*

*Although the court was indeed bored to tears and the defense lawyer was obnoxious, I wanted a fair sentence. Falling asleep while on guard duty during war is a serious offense.*

*I supported the sentence, which was the consensus of the Board, and read the verdict: Reduction to lowest rank, forfeiture of two-thirds of base pay for three months and hard labor without confinement for two months.*

*Court adjourned until tomorrow.*

***4 March 2015***

*Pfc. Adams's marijuana case came before the Board this morning, and fortunately Maj. O'Kelly was not challenged off the court. Today is the fourth time Adams has been summoned without receiving a trial. Last time it was lack of available evidence.*

*Lt. Walker—who is not a lawyer—was the appointed defense counsel. He requested that the President dismiss the case against Pfc. Adams due to negligence of the court to expedite the case, which has caused Adams to suffer mental anguish. The President refused to grant a dismissal, and the trial proceeded.*

*According to a sworn statement by Adams, he unknowingly received the marijuana cigarettes from a friend. He asked for a few cigarettes and did not realize they were pot since they looked like normal cigarettes except that they were crushed. "When the marijuana began to produce weakness in my legs and a sick feeling, I thought I was having another epileptic seizure." When questioned by a dispensary doctor as to whether he had been smoking pot, he said, "Yes, I guess so."*

*The important question raised by the defense counsel was whether or not he was aware of what he was saying to the doctor. Adams said, "I don't remember what I said during this time." Defense counsel stated that Adams was not read Article 31, which protects the right not to answer without a lawyer present.*

*During the Board deliberations, Maj. O'Kelly animatedly pointed out that Adams was charged with "unlawful possession of marijuana," and it was proven that he had same. Whether he was aware that he had marijuana was not the question; therefore, we were left with no choice but to find him guilty as charged. We agreed on the following sentence: Reduction in rank from Pfc. to Pvt. and a verbal reprimand. It was the lightest sentence possible and a fair one. I wasn't convinced that he was truly guilty of a crime.*

Being on the courts-martial boards was emotionally problematic for me. I believe that we all make mistakes and deserve second chances. Both Little and Adams were very young. But according to army regulations, regardless of age, all are accountable for mistakes—especially when you are a low-ranking enlisted soldier. Regrettably, high-ranking officers are sometimes not held accountable for their decisions.

In determining the guilty verdict, Maj. O'Kelly stated that we had no choice but to follow the letter of the law. But was it fair? Was justice served? I'm not sure. I do know that I could never be a trial lawyer or judge. As president of the court, I was overwhelmed by the responsibility to assure a fair trial.

During all these post-Vietnam years, I have never been selected to be on another jury. My military courts-martial have turned out to be my only jury duty.

Although I recognize that we are all accountable for our actions, I had conflicting emotions about judging the young soldiers who had made mistakes. As the Apostle Paul wrote to the Romans, "We have *all* sinned and come short of the glory of God." All of us.

# HONG KONG

***18 March 1967***

*Since December, Lt. Lane McNitt and I have been planning to go to Hong Kong this month. About six weeks ago I turned in my request for R & R to the 61st Medical Battalion, but someone screwed up. Of course, it was not their fault. The lieutenant blamed the inaction on someone in the 43rd Medical Group in Nha Trang, who in turn blamed the 1st Log, etc.*

*As a last resort I went to the 101st Special Services office and asked if they could obtain a seat on the flight with Lt. McNitt to Hong Kong. The young sergeant called to Cam Ranh and made the arrangements for me. It was so simple, and he had no obligation to do this for me.*

*Lane came by this morning to pick me up and introduced to me his friend Lt. Pete Ricca, who was also going to Hong Kong. We were supposed to get on a RMK flight to Cam Ranh, but it was filled. Fortunately, Mr. Barber of RMK was in charge of loading passengers and managed to get us on the plane. Perhaps it was because I had his shopping list for items to buy in Hong Kong.*

*We arrived at the Cam Ranh R & R Center before noon, checked in and were assigned beds for the night. Our flight will leave tomorrow at 1400 hours. Meanwhile, there is nothing to do so I bought a book,*

The Conversion of Chaplain Coen, *and sat in the sun reading.*

*Tonight we went to the Air Force Officers' Club for dinner and returned to the barracks, a tropical building housing 100 men. The wood boards are louvered with spacing to allow airflow and the roof is tin, which reflects some of the sun. I was awake most of the night because of the heat, loud voices and the screen door slamming at all hours.*

***19 March 1967***

*A pretty stewardess handed me a cold towel as soon as I was seated in the Pan Am DC7. From 30,000 feet, Vietnam looks so much better. Three hours later, we arrived in Hong Kong and were escorted from the airport to the R & R Center for a briefing. Afterwards we took a bus to the President Hotel, where Pete, Lane and I were assigned three adjacent rooms.*

*After unpacking we went to the hotel lobby to find Richard Kan, who friends had recommended as the man to take care of us. Mr. Kan owns and operates Peninsula Tailors, located in the lobby of our hotel. There are numerous tailors in Hong Kong, but Mr. Kan can be trusted to make quality clothes at fair prices, according to other 101st officers, who returned to Phan Rang singing his praises.*

*All three of us had measurements made for new clothes. Pete went wild and spent over $500, and Lane's purchases totaled over $250. I came out low for only $166, which included two suits, five shirts and two pairs of shoes—all items handmade by Mr. Kan and his workers.*

*After supper in the hotel coffee shop, we walked around town going into several bars and listening to the music. The Firecracker Bar featured an all-girl rock-and-roll band, which was excellent. It was a long day, and I returned to my room for a hot bath and sleep.*

I have always had problems finding shoes to fit my long, narrow feet. Having custom-made shoes was a dream come true. First, Mr. Kan measured my feet carefully. The next day I returned and he had made a canvas model shoe for me. After I slipped it on, he made further adjustments and told me to return in two days. The result was a pair of loden-green leather—yes, green—and a pair of traditional black, wingtip shoes. I wore the wingtip shoes for several years, but I lost them in subsequent years of moving.

I have just returned from the guest bedroom closet to check on the condition of one of the suits that Mr. Kan made for me nearly fifty years ago. Although snug fitting, the wool and silk jacket in a dark cobalt blue still looks pretty good on me. Inside the jacket the label stitching reveals: "Specially Made for Mr. J. C. Whitener." The slim cut of the jacket and pants was very fashionable in the 1960s. And introducing the retro look, Burberry, the British fashion house, recently advertised "a slim-fit suit with a short, closely fitted jacket and narrow tapered trousers crafted in silk and wool" for $2,295. I thought that perhaps I had held on to this suit because it is stunning and reminds of those wonderful days in Hong Kong when I was young. But as it turns out, it was an investment that increased in value from $50 to $2,295.

***20 March 1967***

*While enjoying the soft, clean, cool sheets, I turned on the radio and found an English-speaking DJ. I was tempted to stay in bed all morning. After a delicious hot bath, I joined Pete and Lane in the coffee shop for breakfast—a chicken liver omelet and hot tea.*

*At 1000 hours, Mr. Kan sent a driver to pick us up to shop at the China Fleet Club, which houses businesses under contract with the U.S. Navy to offer merchandise at reduced prices to military personnel. You can buy anything—china, stereo equipment, cameras, flatware, clothing, jewelry, leather goods and more. I bought a human hair wig for Mother and Seiko watches and cashmere sweaters for my parents and sister. I bought a reel-to-reel tape deck and a leather suit carrier for myself.*

*China Fleet is on Hong Kong Island, and our hotel is across the island in Kowloon. The government is building an underground tunnel to connect the island to the mainland. Meanwhile the only connection is a ferry, which runs every two minutes.*

*Tonight Mr. Kan treated us—14 servicemen—to a 14-course Chinese dinner. As we sat around a large, round table, the feast—*

*wonton soup, spring rolls, sweet and sour pork, roast duck in two courses, eggs with shredded pork, fried beef with oyster sauce, fried freshwater shrimps, fried mushrooms and bamboo shoots, special chicken, fried rice, and an apple toffee dessert—was served on huge platters family style.*

*Our host Paul, one of Mr. Kan's employees, initiated a drinking game with hot sake—a fermented rice drink that smells like kerosene. Paul placed an uncooked chicken head on a saucer and covered it with a cup. He then spun the saucer and when it stopped, he removed the cup. Whoever the chicken beak pointed to was to chug their glass of sake. He spun the beak seven times, and twice the beak pointed to me. Fortunately, I was sitting between Pete and Lane, who graciously took turns drinking the sake for me. The men at our table drank four jugs of the vile liquid.*

*After dinner most of the men walked down the street to a bar, but Pete, Lane, and I returned to our hotel.*

Lane McNitt was a friend for "taking the sake" for me. He was also a good soldier, functioning as training officer of Replacement Training Company, 101st Airborne, 1st Brigade, where he and his men were responsible for passing on information they learned from their jungle fighting to the new arrivals.

Lane did not go out to bars searching for girls, because he was engaged to his high school sweetheart. Upon returning to the States, he planned to enter college to major in police administration. He went to the Hong Kong Police Department and asked for a tour of the facility. He planned to use his photos and information about their operations for a future paper. The Hong Kong police commissioner was impressed with an American soldier using his R & R time to learn about their police operations and invited him home to have dinner with his family.

Lane returned to the States and obtained a degree in criminal justice from the University of California. He retired after twenty-five years with the Secret Service, having served on protection detail for presidents and vice presidents. Unknown to either of us, we were both working in Washington, D.C., at the same time. He is still married to his high school sweetheart.

***21 March 1967***

*My day started at 0700 when I called home and spoke to my family. The time in Hickory was 1800 and everyone was eating supper except brother Ronnie, who was working late during his spring vacation. It was wonderful to hear their voices.*

*Later at breakfast I said to Pete, who was staring at two American girls, "I think I know one of the girls." I couldn't be sure so I walked across the room to her table. It was Kitty Hess, who I last saw at my farewell party, and now by chance I see her 7,000 miles from Fort Knox. She is traveling with a friend, Chickie, who teaches grammar school in Okinawa. Pete and I made a dinner date for tonight.*

*We checked in with Mr. Kan, who made further fittings for our new shoes and suits. I asked him to recommend a place for an authentic Chinese bath.*

*The Chinese bath experience was the highlight of the day. A man led Pete, Lane, and me through a maze of stalls into a room with three couches. We were told to undress and then led naked to a hot, stinking, steaming pool of water. After bathing our bodies, we were motioned to three cots, where an old, fat man scrubbed our bodies with soap—no spot went unscrubbed. Very stimulating.*

*After about 15 minutes, we were led into another room where we were splashed with clean water, and then back to the original room to lie down again on the cots. Six men were waiting for us—two per person. One beat my body with a branch of leaves, while another man gave me a pedicure and manicure. I was feeling great until one man turned me on my stomach and began walking on my back. This pressure triggered a coughing reflex, which finally made the man stop.*

*We were served hot tea and given time to meditate. The elaborate bath ritual involved a total of nine men and each of them asked for a tip for a total of $6.00—well worth the extraordinary experience.*

*Tonight Pete and I took Kitty and Chickie to the Carlton Hotel, which is located on a hilltop offering a splendid view of the harbor. Kitty and I started with snails in garlic butter sauce, followed by soup and chicken Kiev (lots of liquid butter and herbs oozed out when I cut it open with a knife). For dessert I had baked Alaska. I enjoyed the evening catching up with Kitty on our old friends at Knox. We left the Carlton and went dancing at the Firecracker Bar.*

There were no romantic sparks between Kitty and me, and apparently not between Pete and Chickie. Pete didn't suggest or show interest in another double date. Nor did he have a date for any other night. Perhaps he was gay also, but I was afraid to discuss the possibility. I didn't want to go to bars and meet women because I preferred Peter Ricca.

Oh Peter, Peter, Peter, I had such a crush on him. Tall, dark, and handsome. I supposed he will never know how tortured I was being with him those five days in Hong Kong and not expressing my feelings.

Pete Rica was from New York City. Years later, I searched a Manhattan phone book for his name and phone number. There were nearly two dozen listings for Peter Ricca. I didn't call anyone from the list.

***22 March 1967***
*I am confused by the U.S. attitude toward trade with China. There are strict regulations against buying anything here with origin in mainland China, yet the U.S. government sends thousands of military personnel here on leave and R&R where we spend money for products produced in China.*

*Today Pete and I took a tour of Hong Kong Island where we saw the floating village of Aberdeen, the Repulse Bay area, the Tiger Balm Gardens and the refugee shacks. Aberdeen consists of floating houses jammed together for as far as you see. They were a significant contrast to the magnificent homes—including one belonging to movie star William Holden—overlooking Repulse Bay, on the southern tip of Hong Kong Island.*

*While touring the Tiger Balm Gardens, Pete and I were asked for an interview by Welles Hangen, a journalist with* NBC Nightly News. *Being the ham I am, I said, "Sure."*

***23 March 1967***

*At breakfast I listened to Pete's misadventures from last night. After leaving him in the hotel lobby, he decided to go out again. At the Gaslight Bar he talked with a lovely young girl who requested that he buy her out of the bar for $17. She conceded that if she really liked him she would cut the fee to $10, however, that didn't include the fee for over-night. After all, she had a child to support. Pete said, "No thank you," and returned to the hotel alone.*

*I called the R & R office and asked if it would be OK to grant an interview to NBC News. The sergeant strongly advised against the interview and recommended that I obtain permission from the American Consulate.*

*Pete and I went to the China Fleet Club to mail packages home and met Welles Hangen. While waiting for Pete to finish mailing his packages, I called the American Consulate office and was told a man was on his way to talk to us. After waiting for over an hour, we began the interview with Hagen without official approval. Shortly into the interview, a Navy Commander arrived and wanted to know what was going on. After asking Hangen a few questions, he gave us his approval to continue.*

*The reason we were being cautious is that in the past men have impersonated reporters who in fact represented radical, protest groups, who would use the interview with GIs for propaganda purposes. I personally felt that Hagen was genuine because I listened to him interview a chaplain and Navy captain before our interview began.*

*In our briefing before the camera was turned on, he said he would only ask questions about our tourist experiences in Hong Kong. Not true. When the taping began, he threw in two questions we weren't expecting. One was "Has anyone tried to draw you into political discussions in Hong Kong?" (We had been warned to avoid all discussions of politics here.) The other question: "There has been talk from Red China that the Americans are building up*

*Hong Kong into an American base for the further take-over of Southeast Asia. Have you heard anything like this?"*

*Answer to both questions: "No." Hagen said that if the tape was used it would be shown on TV news within the next two weeks.*

*Tonight Pete and I had dinner on the 18th floor of the President Hotel, which offered a grand view of Kowloon and the harbor. Our last night in Hong Kong.*

I told my parents to watch *NBC Nightly News* the next two weeks to see the interview. Apparently, the interview was never aired. In retrospect I don't think it was newsworthy, since it only consisted of two GIs saying "no" to interesting questions.

Three years later, Welles Hangen and four other journalists were declared missing after Communist forces ambushed their vehicle in Cambodia. In 1991, Cambodia allowed a NBC news team to return to the village where he was last seen. The villagers reported that Hangen was beaten to death. Tests confirmed that a recovered skeleton was his. He was buried in Arlington National Cemetery with a twenty-one-gun salute.

***24 March 1967***

*I was up early to catch the 0830 flight back to Vietnam. At the airport I called Kitty and Chickie to say goodbye. The last five days in Hong Kong had flown by.*

*As I boarded the Pan Am flight, I dreaded returning to Vietnam. But I had time to re-acclimate during the flight to Cam Ranh Bay and the 30-mile, dusty, rough ride in an Army truck back to Phan Rang.*

I will always remember those five days of adventure in Hong Kong and, most of all, Peter Ricca. Our dinner at the President Hotel with the grand view of Kowloon was our last time together. The occasion had all the makings for a romantic evening, but it was not to be. I wanted Peter Ricca to come to my room where I would touch his body all over, and he would tenderly kiss me. It was a fantasy not fulfilled. Why didn't I ask him? Because I was petrified to think of that possibility.

If only times had been different, and I had been able to be honest, both with myself and Peter, Kitty, and others. But the year was 1967, and if I had admitted my homosexuality, I could have been court-martialed. I couldn't confide in anyone. I kept my feelings, tortured as I was, inside my head…safe from the military.

# IN COMMUNIST HANDS

***25 March 1967***
*I made the big decision today. There is no turning back; the result is irrevocable. What wasn't performed on the eighth day after my birth (and in the Jewish tradition) was accomplished today thanks to the talented hands of Marv Youkilis and Gene Fishman.*

For whatever reasons (I never discussed this with my parents), I was not circumcised. In 1942 in the South, it wasn't the medical norm to cut an infant's foreskin. So I grew up with a foreskin and other physical characteristics—big feet, skinny body—all of which I wished were different.

Twenty-five years later, I am in hot, sticky, dusty Vietnam, where I took at least three showers a day. (After all, cleanliness is next to godliness.) Of course, I was lucky to have this luxury and it seems wasteful, but I was not aware of a shortage of water. Several times a week army trucks would deliver potable water to fill the five-gallon cans and our two-barrel shower. The water temperature could be chilly for morning showers, but later in the day the sun heated the water in the barrels.

It was during one of my showers that I saw a soldier shaving his pubic hair. (In the 1960s, shaving the genital area was not in fashion.) After noticing my acute interest in his unusual activity, he explained he was shaving in preparation for a circumcision.

To build up my courage, I observed several circumcisions on young military men by our two Jewish physicians, Marv and Gene. They were not looking for an excuse for a bris celebration, nor to convert fine young Christian boys to the Jewish faith. I think they performed their surgical magic because they were bored with routine morning sick calls.

And there were valid reasons for adult male circumcision: hygiene, cancer prevention, and other medical issues. In my case, Marv and Gene medically justified the procedure due to moderate phimosis, but my primary motivation was to look like most other American guys . . . down there.

I showered and shaved to prep myself before nervously presenting myself on the dispensary's surgical table. With gloved hands, Marv immediately began turning my penis in various positions as if looking for something. Finally I said, "Marv, that is all there is." He laughed. It was strange having an army colleague handling my penis.

Traditionally, the only anesthesia given the Jewish infant by the mohel is a drop of sweet wine on his lips. Although Marv was a physician, a non-physician can conduct the ritual. And in Exodus I read that Zipporah, Moses's wife, took a sharp stone and circumcised her son. Given the choice, I decided to go the knife route.

"The injection of the topical anesthetic under the skin of your penis is going to hurt a little," he said. Marv was right, but it was the only painful part of the procedure. The operation from beginning to end took less than thirty minutes. In the ancient tradition, which is much faster for an infant, the mohel sucked the blood away. I can assure you that Marv didn't.

Seven days later, I took out the stitches. My penis was back to normal functioning sans foreskin.

Before the surgery began, I requested that Marv keep my foreskin and place it in formaldehyde to preserve it. He obliged. From the time of the surgery until I left Vietnam I kept my foreskin on my desk in a glass bottle and used it as a paperweight. Visitors to my office were fascinated. Soldiers would pick up the bottle, shake it, and watch in awe as "it" floated down, reminiscent of the old-fashioned snow scenes in other paperweights. After a while I would casually say, "You are playing with my foreskin." It became a conversation piece.

Why did I keep my foreskin? Perhaps I remembered the biblical text from Samuel in which King Saul told David that the price for his bride was one hundred Philistine foreskins. I would only need ninety-nine more—and the desire to marry a woman.

Three months later it was finally time to leave Vietnam. I had few worldly possessions to pack up and take home: a Montagnard crossbow and spears, a tape deck, peasant shirt and pants, and a deactivated hand grenade. I debated how to safely pack the special bottle for the long journey back to America. If the bottle broke the formaldehyde would ruin the other packaged contents.

In the last-minute frenzy of packing and saying goodbyes, I forgot my foreskin. The rest is history. Eventually, the North Vietnamese took over Phan Rang in their push south toward Saigon. And I can only imagine what happened to my foreskin. I do believe that one way or another, it probably remains in Communist hands.

# LIGHT IN THE LOAFERS

***11 April 1967***

*This week three officers and all but four of the corpsman of the 221st Dispensary departed for Cam Ranh Bay. Spec. Martin remained here as my assistant. In addition to his assigned job as ward attendant, he voluntarily began helping me with patients several weeks ago. He is an excellent worker, and requested to stay here as my optometric assistant. Although he was married, other corpsmen joked about Martin's sexual proclivities: "Did Martin take care of you last night?" "No, I fought him off."*

*I learned this morning that he was in the Air Force hospital with a fractured mandible. It seems that last evening he went to the Air Force Enlisted Men's Club where he met Airman Dumfries, who was celebrating his last night in Vietnam. They drank heavily. After the club closed, Martin asked Dumfries to walk back with him, and he agreed to walk halfway to our base camp. Somewhere in between the club and base, they sat down in a field and had a few more beers. According to Dumfries, he passed out and woke up to find Martin in his pants. Dumfries picked up a rock and bashed Martin's face, fracturing his mandible, and in turn Martin struck back, giving Dumfries a six-inch cut on his face, which required stitches.*

*Later in the day Martin returned to the dispensary on his way to the field hospital in Nha Trang for treatment. I could hardly recognize him with all the facial cuts, swelling and bruises.*

*The Criminal Investigation Command, commonly known as the CID, will investigate the sodomy charge.*

***18 April 1967***

*Col. Novick, the towering 250-pound commander of Phan Rang sub area, came today to tell Mahoney to notify the CID immediately concerning the sodomy charges against Martin. (Our unit is under 1st Log, 61st Medical Battalion and assigned to 101st Airborne.) This demand from Novick doesn't make sense because our dispensary's administration unit is in Cam Ranh, and McNeely is not our CO. Why didn't Novick go to the CID directly?*

*Mahoney tried to contact the CID by telephone, but couldn't get through. He then asked me to go to the CID, which I did. The warrant officer in charge couldn't understand what all the fuss was about since Dumfries had left for the States and did NOT press charges.*

Although we didn't have a discussion about sexuality, I think the reason Martin asked to stay in Phan Rang and work for me was that he sensed I was gay. I deeply regret I didn't offer Martin any support during this difficult time. Empathy for him could have caused suspicion about my own sexuality.

Ironically, Mahoney asked *me* to go to the CID to inquire about the investigation of alleged homosexual conduct by my enlisted assistant, and I don't know why I agreed to go. I had to be careful at the CID office and not give them any reason to question my association with Martin. I knew that accusations of homosexuality could end my military career.

Historically, the military discharged homosexuals—even though celibate—with a blue discharge that meant they were undesirable and unfit for military service. Later the "blue" was replaced with a "dishonorable" discharge for soldiers found guilty of same-sex behavior.

During the time I was in Vietnam, CID investigations for homosexual activity—even between consenting adults—led to a dishonorable discharge. In Martin's case, the charge was sodomy under Article 125*, which the military defined as "engaging in unnatural carnal copulation with another person of the same or opposite sex or with an animal." The unnatural copulation includes oral or anal sex.

In 1975, Air Force Tech. Sgt. Leonard Matlovich challenged the military's discrimination policies in court. He agreed to be a test case because he had an exemplary military career and wanted to remain in the military as an openly gay man. He had received a Bronze Star for meritorious service and a Purple Heart for shrapnel wounds during one of his three tours in Vietnam. Matlovich hand-delivered a letter to his commanding officer and when he asked, "What does this mean?" replied, "It means Brown versus the Board of Education." Powerful words. I was never willing to risk it all as Matlovich did.

Matlovich had sought the advice of D.C. activist Frank Kameny to proceed with his plans. (In 1976, I invited Kameny to speak at the University of Chapel Hill for the first Southeastern Gay Conference.) Kameny and Matlovich were true pioneers in the advancement of gay rights and heroes to me.

During Matlovich's administrative discharge hearing, an Air Force attorney asked him if he would sign a document pledging to "never practice homosexuality again" in exchange for being allowed to remain in the military. After replying no, he was recommended for a General discharge, which was later upgraded to Honorable.

He sued the military, and five years later U.S. District Court Judge Gesell ordered him reinstated and promoted. The air force offered Matlovich a financial settlement to include back pay, future pay, and pension, which he accepted. I understand this decision to settle, because his future promotion and career path would otherwise be tarnished by the lawsuit.

---

* Article 125 remains in the Uniform Code of Military Justice, along with the ban on bestiality.

Matlovich died of AIDS at age 44 and is buried in the Congressional Cemetery in Washington, D.C. The black reflective marble tombstone is nameless as a memorial to all gay vets. On the tombstone are etched two pink triangles, which were the symbols the Nazi regime forced homosexuals to wear, with the phases "Never Again" and "Never Forget." The inscription below the triangles reads: *When I was in the military, they gave me a medal for killing two men and a discharge for loving one.*

In 1992, I was hopeful when candidate Bill Clinton promised to lift the ban on homosexuals in the military. In 1993, facing strong opposition from the military, he agreed to the infamous compromise policy "Don't ask, don't tell" (DADT). In theory DADT would prohibit military personnel from discriminating against or harassing closeted homosexual or bisexual service members. Superiors were to not initiate questioning or investigation about military service member's sexual orientation without first having witnessed or received credible evidence. Service members were prohibited from disclosing their sexual orientation or homosexual relationships. If I had disclosed that I was gay, I would have been investigated. Over fourteen thousand members of the military were investigated and discharged because of their sexual orientation during the eighteen years of DADT.

In 2007, I was elated when candidate Barack Obama committed to ending "Don't ask, don't tell." Three years later Congress passed a bipartisan bill repealing the policy, providing it would stay in place until President Obama, the Secretary of Defense, and the Chairman of the Joint Chiefs of Staff all agreed that the repeal of DADT would not harm military readiness. Secretary of Defense Gates and Joint Chief of Staff Mullen concurred to support the repeal. In remarks before the Senate Armed Forces Committee, Admiral Mullen stated, "It is the right thing to do." Republican Senator Susan Collins, who was key to overturning DADT, stated: "Today for the first time in history, we will welcome the service of any qualified individual who is willing to put on the uniform of our country." Democratic Senator Ron Wyden said, "If you love this country enough to risk your life for it, you shouldn't have to hide who you are."

Gay and lesbian soldiers did hide their sexuality for sixty-three years after President Truman signed Executive Order 9981 stating: "There shall be equality of treatment and opportunity for all persons in the armed services without regard to race, color, religion, or national origin." While Truman boldly ended the military's racial segregation, he did not end discrimination against gay and lesbian soldiers. Gay soldiers were denied "equality of treatment and opportunity." At last, on September 20, 2011, the Department of Defense changed regulations to no longer include homosexual conduct as grounds for administrative separation. It was a long time coming.

With the DOD decision, my mind was flooded with memories of Vietnam and Martin. Thinking about all the lives ruined and the careers destroyed saddens me. For the thousands of soldiers who were discharged under former policies, the Department of Defense now has an administrative process to upgrade veterans discharged for being gay. I hope this process is fast and effective for all gay veterans to receive their honorable discharge and to be recognized for their service to our country.

The *Asheville Citizens-Times* interviewed me as part of an article on the end of DADT. I told the reporter that I was lucky to not have been caught and kicked out of the military because I was gay during my entire twenty-three-year career.

The military was more than a nine-to-five job: It was a unique comradeship often making it difficult to hide my homosexuality. In Vietnam I worked and lived with my colleagues at all times and was not able to share who I really was or talk about my sexual conflicts. Friendships were superficial.

Surely men in my unit sensed that I was gay. Recently I asked a colleague who served with me in the 221st Dispensary if he—or other soldiers—thought I was gay. He responded, "I'm sure we thought you were a little too much on the feminine side and sometimes a little light in the loafers, but as for being gay, I don't think so. I remember you planting flowers in front of your tent. Looking back, I'm not shocked."

"Light in the loafers." I find the description funny for someone who wore jungle boots every day. I didn't even own a pair of loafers, but I caught his drift.

As my former colleague unintentionally reminded me, I have often struggled with the concept of femininity, which always weighed on my mind in the masculine military world. When I was growing up, my parents called me by my middle name, Carroll. When I went away to college and later entered the military, I chose to use my first name, John, to escape the feminine-sounding Carroll. From my earliest memory, I was aware that I was expected to hide my feminine side. I had no ability for sports, and my efforts to throw a football resulted in snickering or snide remarks. Of course, it didn't help my image when I became the first male cheerleader in my high school. (One of our cheers positioned me in the center of a chorus line of high-kicking girls. Yes, I kicked with the girls.) My cousin Wade defended me when tough guys threatened me.

My paranoia about my feminine side continued throughout my military career. I was always conscious of my voice inflection, laughter, and choice of words. Since early childhood, I learned that there were consequences for appearing effeminate and being labeled a "sissy." I tried to blend in with the rest of the boys. I developed a sense of humor so that whenever I told clever stories or jokes, people laughed with me instead of at me.

Luckily, I was never beaten up, as was Spec. Martin. I regret my lack of compassion when he returned to the dispensary, bruised and broken. I have never forgotten him, and I hope that he is doing well.

# INCONVENIENT TRUTHS

***13 April 1967***

*Since the military engineers moved the camp's main generator several months ago, the dispensary has had surges of electricity and power failures. We have been relying on our own 15-kilowatt generator to run our dispensary's lights, equipment, and air-conditioning units. My disgruntlement increased when I learned that there is a huge hydroelectric power plant about ten miles west of here. We can't use it because the VC destroy the power lines each time they are repaired.*

*In the past week our generator broke down and since it's the only one of its kind in the area, the repairman doesn't know how to fix it. Among other inconveniences, I can't examine patients without electricity.*

*Last week I examined two patients who are Army-trained bakers. But they don't bake, because they don't have all the necessary equipment. I asked, "What do you do all day?"*

*One soldier replied, "I pull maintenance on my equipment." How inconvenient for a baker to be without his oven.*

*Breakage of eyeglasses is a common occurrence. I have been told by soldiers that their company commander gives them a hard time when they ask to return to base camp for new eyeglasses. I understand losing a man from the field a few days affects operations, but a soldier who can't see, can't accurately aim his rifle. Another patient had more than an inconvenience of broken glasses to cope with—gonorrhea of the eye. Previously I had only seen textbook pictures of this condition. It is a gory sight.*

*It hasn't rained in three months and the parched topsoil relocates, forming a layer of red dirt on my bed and everything else in the tent. In the past two days, the amount of dirt and flying objects has increased, because medevac helicopters have landed next to my tent. If Jim and I hadn't held onto the tent posts for dear life, the entire tent would have blown away. What is annoying is that the helicopters have a designated helipad, but the pilots mistakenly land on the flattened, graded area that was designated as the site for a new dispensary, which has never been built. Another inconvenience.*

*At 1630 I called the 43rd Medical Group in Nha Trang and asked about my promotion orders. I was supposed to be promoted to Captain two days ago, but inconveniently my battalion command couldn't find the paperwork. I was informed that the orders were cut two days ago and were forwarded to my medical battalion in Cam Ranh. I am now a Captain according to Special Orders #96, paragraph number two. I immediately put on my silver tracks and went to supper.*

I have been asked what was the hardest part of my Vietnam tour. My answer is, "Giving up the conveniences of everyday life: running water, flushing toilets, telephone, and television." I am embarrassed to admit the pettiness of this truth, when I know soldiers who endured abhorrent conditions fighting and dying in rice paddies and jungles. Compared to these soldiers, I realize that my tour was a picnic. I was lucky.

In my diary I am complaining about dirt on my tent bed—at least I had a tent to sleep in. When I returned from Vietnam, I vowed that I would never go camping again. After all, I had lived in a tent for a year, and the idea of voluntarily giving up modern conveniences to camp was not my idea of fun.

It took me five years to get over my self-imposed ban on camping. In the summer of 1973, I bought a two-person tent and camped across the country from the mountains of North Carolina to the coast of California. The drive up the coast on Highway 1 from San Diego to San Francisco was magical. I camped near Monterey and attended the Jazz Festival, where I heard Dizzy Gillespie and Carmen McRae.

The truth is that camping did not remind me of Vietnam and was not inconvenient because the other person in my tent happened to be a boyfriend.

# THE HEX

***27 April 1967***

*I met Spec.4 Thompson, a 47-year old medic, when he came to our clinic. His missing teeth brought him in to see Jim and his vision problem brought him to me for an eye examination. Jim worked on his mouth, and I worked on his eyes. The result was a new dental plate and three new pairs of eyeglasses. In gratitude for our helping him to chew his food and see what he was eating, he offered to build us a new two-person tropical house to replace our sleeping quarters. I didn't hesitate to agree. I am tired of living in one half of the tent where our medical supplies are stored.*

*Since Thompson told me he could build tropical houses, I didn't see a need to supervise the construction. And Jim wasn't available because he was on R & R in Bangkok. To begin with he built eight sides to fit on the already existing hexagon-shaped cement foundation. When he discovered that the eight sections didn't fit on the foundation, he used six of the eight prefabricated sides anyway. The result was smaller side panels, which wasted precious feet of floor space and created gaps for rain, wind and dust to penetrate. The hexagon house looks ridiculous: the walls are nearly twice as tall as the diameter of the foundation. But we do have a new tin roof over our heads.*

*Jim returned today from Bangkok intoxicated—not unusual. He came into my office with a beer, which he spilled on the floor as he rattled off a series of questions to find out what was going on with our sleeping quarters. Everyone who sees the house throws in disparaging remarks.*

*Jim named the new structure "Whitener's Folly." I call it the "Hex."*

The wooden tropical building seemed a smart idea to protect our sleeping area from fierce winds which blew dust over the denuded and parched earth and into our old tent. Furthermore, the monsoon season that followed frequently flooded our base camp and my tent.

I should have been suspicious of Thompson's building skills when he told me he was also a trained army medic. His age, forty-seven, and his low rank were indicators that he had screwed up during his military career. I should have asked him why an army medic was building tropical houses.

Living in the ludicrous Hex for the next two months did not put a hex on my life. The unique structure was a one-of-a-kind architectural mess, but I was a mess, too. The strange wooden house was an improvement over sleeping in one half of our dispensary's supply tent. The sound of rain on the tin roof took me back in time to sleepovers at Granny Whitener's house, where I remember the musty, crunchy hay-stuffed mattress and the comforting sound of gentle rain on the tin roof.

# GOING BERSERK

***28 April 1967***
*Today Willie Edwards went berserk. No one knows why he began firing his M16 rifle in the barracks. One guy heard shots and decided to jump under the bed until he noticed bullet holes in his shower shoes under his bed. Willie then walked from the barracks to the outdoor movie theater where the soldiers were watching a cowboy movie. As he fired his rifle, real bullets whizzed through the air as the movie kept rolling. Amazingly Willie failed to shoot anyone; perhaps he wasn't trying. He was apprehended and sent to the LBJ jail in Long Benh.*

Although I didn't personally know Willie Edwards, I can understand how war, personal issues, and religious conflicts can cause a soldier to go crazy.

In 2009, Maj. Nidal Malik Hasan, an army psychiatrist, killed 13 soldiers and injured 30 people in a Fort Hood Soldier Readiness Processing Center. Unlike Brown, Hasan shot to kill. Why?

Hasan was born in Arlington County, Virginia, and in 1984 attended Wakefield High School, which for years I walked past to the subway station to go to work. He attended the officer basic training program at Fort Sam Houston, where I went to basic training, and was commissioned in 1997, the year I retired from the army. Our paths almost crossed at Walter Reed Army Medical Center (WRAMC), where my reserve unit trained and he completed his residency in psychiatry. And we both have a master's degree in public health. Six degrees of separation?

During his internship at WRAMC, Hasan began counseling soldiers who had returned from the Middle East with post-traumatic stress disorder. Reportedly, he was horrified by the stories, and in addition, was harassed about his Muslim religion and beliefs. The shootings occurred a few days before his deployment to Afghanistan.

Hasan allegedly shouted "Allahu Akbar," or "God is great," as he began the carnage at Fort Hood. How did he use his religious beliefs to justify killing American soldiers? I understand how religious beliefs can affect one's life because religion and Bible verses certainly shaped my thinking about the world and my place in it.

Growing up, I did not question the biblical scriptures because I was told that God inspired *every* word. At that time I didn't know that the stories of the Old Testament were written in Hebrew, then translated into Latin and Greek and eventually English. Perhaps "lost in translation" helps explain the story from chapter 19 of Genesis, which is used by fundamentalists to condemn homosexuality. The Bible tells us that two angels (disguised as men) were visiting Lot in Sodom when all the town's men surrounded Lot's house and demanded to have sex with his visitors. Instead Lot offered the Sodomites his two daughters. God destroyed Sodom and Gomorrah with burning sulfur for its evilness. Later in the nineteenth chapter we learn that Lot had sex with his two daughters, who bore him children. What father offers up his daughters for sex? And later has sex with the daughters? Out of this terrible story comes the biblical teaching that homosexuality is a sin punishable by burning in hell. My take on Sodom and Lot's daughters is that gang rape and incest are both immoral, whether heterosexual or homosexual.

I will never forget the condemnation of the Old Testament scriptures preached in the church I knew as a teenager. But years later, I was reassured when I realized that Jesus never condemned homosexuality. For all the laws of the Prophets in the Bible, Jesus summed up what was really important: "Love the Lord your God with all your heart and with all your soul and all your mind. This is the first and greatest commandment. And the second is like it: Love your neighbor as yourself."

I believe that loving our neighbor includes our gay, transgender, black, brown, straight, and Muslim neighbor. We are to love without a qualifier. Now that is berserk.

# MAY DAY

***1 May 1967***

*A couple of nights ago the VC blew up the petroleum pipeline between Phan Rang and the beach. The explosion killed two Vietnamese prostitutes who were passengers in a jeep with civilian personnel from the American Alaska Barge.*

*Not a May Day celebration**, but in honor of the 101st Support Battalion's sergeant major, we had a special dinner tonight at the mess hall complete with tablecloths, wine, and waitresses dressed in the festive, traditional ao dai. We toasted him, the President of the United States, and all the sergeants major in the Army.*

*On our way back from supper Jim said, "There's going to be an alert in about 10 minutes." Not taking the alert seriously, he went to his clinic and I went to bed in the Hex.*

*Some time later, I was awakened by a blast, which didn't bother me because we hear blasts all the time. A minute later there was another blast, and Jim came running into the Hex. "It's for real," he said as he grabbed his helmet and flak vest. I jumped out of bed and did the same.*

---

* May Day was once a pagan religious holiday with singing and dancing. As an eighth-grade student, I remember weaving brightly colored ribbons around the Maypole.

*We ran to the connex , picked up our pistols, and rushed back to crouch behind our sandbagged wall at the Hex. During this time we heard the alert siren and saw other soldiers hurrying to their posts.*

*After ten minutes and with no further explosions, we figured the alert must have been a practice alert and not an attack. Later I learned the explosions came from dynamite thrown onto the parade field to simulate mortars.*

Why was I so cavalier in describing a possible attack on our base? I prayed that I would be safe, and I didn't worry.

Although there was repeated enemy action around the perimeter, our base camp was never attacked. I believed I was safe because the 101st and ROK (Republic of South Korea) troops guarded our perimeter. The ROK forces had a high kill ratio of the enemy and were feared as tough combatants. The ROK soldiers arrived shortly after U.S. marines in 1965 and fought until the end in 1973.

I didn't live that year in terror that our camp would be overrun with enemy soldiers. The fear I lived with daily was that someone would find out my secret.

# DIVIDED COUNTRY

***14 May 1967***

*When I was at officers' basic training at Fort Sam, the number of soldiers killed in Vietnam was less than 300, and the U.S. was in an advisory capacity to the people of South Vietnam. All that changed.*

*While senators, housewives, businessmen, students, beatniks, and everyone else have argued pro and con concerning the U.S. fighting in Vietnam, 7,826 American men have been killed. After all these deaths and billions spent in material, we are no closer to the end of this war. An area cleared of VC one day can be infiltrated with just as many VC the next day or a week later. This war is fruitless.*

*According to the* Stars and Stripes, *last month there were organized demonstrations across the U.S. In New York City there was an antiwar rally with 125,000 demonstrators. Washington, D.C.: 100,000. San Francisco: 55,000.*

*In response to the demonstrations and events, the NYC fire department subsequently organized a parade to support the fighting men in Vietnam. Today 63,000 people marched in NYC in the eight-hour parade. Two skydivers with American flags attached to their chutes landed in Central Park where a month earlier a flag was burned.*

I had read about the flag burning in the *Stars and Stripes* newspaper, but I didn't know that draft cards were also burned—a far bigger story to me.

In the 1960s, the military draft was an issue that divided young, old, black, white, rich, and poor Americans. Thousands of young men fled to Canada rather than go to war in Vietnam. In 1973, as the Vietnam War was coming to an end, the Selective Service announced the end of the draft. Seven years later, President Jimmy Carter reinstituted the requirement that young men register with the Selective Service System within thirty days of their eighteenth birthday. And although no one has been drafted since the end of the Vietnam War, this requirement is still in effect today for only young men. While gender equality has been addressed in the military services, Congress has not mandated that women register for the draft.

In 1967, our military could not fight the Vietnam War without draftees. Young people's refusal to be drafted was an amazingly brave strategy to potentially stop the war. Protests against the draft eventually led to an all-volunteer military.

I learned that Gary Eugene Rader, an Army Reservist, who while wearing his U.S. Army Special Forces uniform, including the smart-looking green beret, burned his draft card at Sheep Meadow in Central Park. Two days later he wrote a letter of resignation to his company commander. For his seditious acts he was arrested and charged for mutilating his draft card and unauthorized wearing of his uniform. He was the only person arrested that day in Central Park. In a letter to the *New York Review*, Rader stated that he could no longer remain in the military and live with his conscience. He went on to set up draft-resistance organizations across the country and was continually jailed with other protesters.

During this same period, I realized that the war in Vietnam was unwinnable and immoral. We were fighting a conventional war against guerrilla warfare; bombing innocent civilians; inflating the number of war dead to mislead the public that we were winning; supporting a corrupt South Vietnamese government; using billions of taxpayers' dollars for South Vietnam infrastructure; burning villages composed of old men, women, and children; and causing hundreds of thousands of deaths and casualties.

I shared my antiwar views with only a few friends. But I was never willing to go to prison for my beliefs. I admire Rader for living his truth regardless of the consequences.

In 1971, while stationed in San Antonio, Texas, I attended the F.T.A—"Fuck the Army"—antiwar event. Among the thousands in the audience, I maintained my anonymity. Jane Fonda and Donald Sutherland headlined the show, which was aimed at soldiers to try to convince us to speak up in opposition to the war. I do remember Jane Fonda using the "F" word, but I have no other memory of the content of the show. Jane Fonda is reviled yet today by some veterans and labeled a traitor. I don't share that view. She was right about how wrong the Vietnam War was.

I never demonstrated against the war, but I did speak up later during the gay rights movement, which happened simultaneously with the antiwar movement. In 1969, gay men and women fought back against repeated police raids at the Stonewall Inn, a gay bar in New York City. That resistance was the genesis of the gay rights movement in the U.S.

The 1960s and '70s were a time of profound social unrest and public polarization. Our country witnessed not only gay rights and antiwar demonstrations, but also the beginning of movements for civil rights, women's rights, and the environment. It was a heady time, in which demonstrators demanded equal rights for all. And it lit a fire within me while a master's student at the University of North Carolina and continued during my twenty years in the D.C. area.

# BRONZE STAR

***16 May 1967***

*Today I found out that Capt. Youkilis had submitted paperwork for a Bronze Star medal for meritorious service for Gene, Ron, Jim, and me. The paperwork was submitted to Ltc. Sunday and forwarded to General Matheson (101st Airborne), who approved, then forwarded to 61st Medical Battalion, where it stopped because Col. Irwin disapproved the recommendation.*

*The award justification described how "Lt. Whitener set up the first Optometry Clinic and supply of prescription eyeglasses in Phan Rang through his own initiative since he had found to his dismay that his equipment had been lost in route from CONUS."*

*After Gen. Matheson signed the recommendation, Col. Irwin had the audacity to attach the following to the original: "Even though this individual was a good worker and he did a good job, his actions do not justify recommendation for the Bronze Star. Recommend USARV Certificate be awarded."*

*Several months prior, Col. Irwin was acutely aware that I jumped the normal chain of command when I wrote Col. Greene in the Pentagon about not having any clinic equipment and my battalion not helping me. He was not pleased then and now he has the last word.*

The Bronze Star (BS) medal is the third-highest honor awarded by the U.S. military and is differentiated from the Silver Star, which is awarded for heroism while under fire. The BS recipient is selected at the discretion of the commanding officer for conduct away from the battlefield. The individual can receive the award for meritorious achievement or service accomplished with distinction. Col. Irvin addressed the issue of meritorious achievement with his dismissive remarks: *Individual was a good worker and did a good job.*

Some five months after leaving Vietnam, I received a telephone call from the CO's office telling me to report to the Fort Bragg hospital commander. My colleagues agreed to see my patients while I went to headquarters. To my dismay, the CO presented me with a Certificate of Achievement from the 1st Logistical Command, which read:

> In recognition of meritorious performance of duty during the period August 1966 to July 1967. He successfully achieved all his objectives in working for the support of the counterinsurgency program against communism in the Republic of Vietnam. Through his energetic and diligent actions, Lieutenant Whitener accomplished superb results and earned for himself the respect and admiration of all his associates. He brought great credit to himself, the 1st Logistical Command, and the military service.

Not exactly a Bronze Star. And while granting the Certificate of Achievement, Col. Irving had managed to insult me. He got my rank wrong and the certificate was a nondescript, "fill in the name" boilerplate form. The certificate should have been designated BS—not as in "Bronze Star," but as in "bull"—because that's exactly what it was.

Although it would have been nice to be recognized for my work, I'm not sure I deserved the Bronze Star. I did receive the Vietnam Service Medal, and wore it on my uniform during the remainder of my military career. Everyone who served more than thirty days in Vietnam and was attached to an organization participating in ground support operations received this medal. Recently I reread my official discharge papers from active duty after Operation Desert Shield/Storm, which stated that I was awarded the National Defense Service Medal with a Bronze Service Star. For reasons unknown, I never received this medal, which is awarded to all who serve honorably on active duty during war. Because I served during two wars, I am entitled to wear a bronze star on the ribbon to denote the second award, the Bronze Service Star. I am ordering this ribbon online. Although it measures only three-sixteenths of an inch, finally I am getting a—if not the—bronze star.

Small, but perhaps appropriate. After all, size isn't everything.

# DINNER PARTY

***19 May 1967***

*Today is Uncle Ho Chi Minh's birthday. Instead of building for the future, he is spending all his energy and money on war, which is causing the death of thousands of his countrymen and the destruction of his land. I can't understand why he doesn't focus on improving the economy and educating the population. Is it to rid South Vietnam of Yankee imperialists? To unite Vietnam? If not that, then what?*

*Several incidents around Phan Rang might be related to the celebration of Uncle Ho's day. At 1300 there were several shots fired into the swimming area at the air force section of the Phan Rang Beach. No one was injured and later reports indicate that it was a Vietnamese soldier trying to shoot the buoy. In another incident a soldier was shot in the arm while guarding our perimeter.*

*It was not billed as an Uncle Ho party, but Thomas Hannum, M.D., invited me to dinner at his villa in downtown Phan Rang. I met Dr. Hannum as a patient when he came to the clinic with his broken glasses. He is in his 30s, married with children, and is a small-town general practitioner from Utah. He volunteered—through the Volunteer Physicians for Vietnam—to work two months at the civilian-run Vietnamese province hospital.*

*At the dinner were also two physicians from the U.S. Air Force, Dr. Hamilton and Dr. and Mrs. Trinh. Dr. Trinh is the head of the Phan Rang Provincial Hospital and a capable doctor, according to Tom. His lovely Vietnamese wife, Nhat, spoke French but understands English.*

*The evening was enjoyable and afforded me a change of routine. It is the first time I've been in Phan Rang village after the 6 PM curfew. I returned safely to base camp.*

It was a lovely dinner party attended by fascinating people. I don't recall any mention of Ho Chi Minh's birthday. Like many American soldiers, I was ignorant of the history of Vietnam and the historical importance of Ho Chi Minh. Of course he wanted to rid South Vietnam of the U.S. soldiers, just as he successfully ran the French out. And although he would not live to see it, Vietnam would be reunited.

Fifty years after the dinner party, I called Dr. Tom Hannum and asked him why he volunteered to serve in the Phan Rang hospital. He told me that two years prior to Vietnam he volunteered his services in Africa, where he met Albert Schweitzer. His experience there changed his life. "But why leave your practice, wife and young children to provide medical services in Vietnam?" I asked.

"Because I wanted to give back. I learned from my parents who were exceedingly kind," he said.

After the dinner, I never saw Dr. Trinh again, but I learned that after the fall of Saigon in 1975, the Communist government imprisoned him. After over a year in prison, he was sent to a re-education labor camp for three years. Like thousands of Vietnamese, Dr. Trinh escaped from Vietnam with his wife and three of his children. In 1979, the family immigrated to the U.S., where he practiced medicine in Kansas and is now retired.

Tom Hannum shared the villa with a British physician, Henry Hamilton. The previous year Hamilton responded to a newspaper article in which the U.S. Secretary of State asked NATO allies to send civilian doctors to Vietnam. He visited the American embassy in London and volunteered his service. After months of delays with bureaucratic offices, he completed his security clearance and signed a contract with the International Rescue Committee, and he was assigned to the Phan Rang Provincial Hospital. In addition to surgical hospital duties, Dr. Hamilton took on the public health challenge of screening and treating the prostitutes at the Strip in an effort to reduce the high rate of VD among American GIs.

Dr. Hamilton's work at the Strip was my first exposure to public health in action. He began to monitor and treat the prostitutes by convincing the hamlet chiefs to enforce the program. He also persuaded local air force personnel to provide medical supplies.

At this time I didn't recognize a future career in public health. But I was impressed with his accomplishments through community outreach and partnership with local government. I would use these collaborative principles in my public health career in Washington, D.C.

# ALMOST FAREWELL

***22 May 1967***

*A month or so before my anticipated departure from Vietnam, I was honored along with twenty-two other men and one woman at a Hail and Farewell dinner at the 101st Officers' Club. After dinner, each person was called before Lt. Col. Sunday for gifts: a 101st Airborne white silk scarf with the Screaming Eagle insignia and the unit's swagger stick with our engraved name. Regrettably, my surname was misspelled and the initial "L" is incorrect, but I appreciated the mementos.*

*The 22-inch wooden mahogany swagger stick is silver-capped with an engraved screaming eagle with the following inscription:*

*1st Brigade 101st Airborne Division*
*Diplomats/Warriors*
*Vietnam*
*CPT J. L. Whitner*

*As each man came forward, he received a loud "Him, him, fuck him" chorus, disregarding the female in the group. After a few "Him choruses," it got old, but they continued for 23 times. Jim Mahoney received two "Hims"—one for his handlebar mustache, and one from Col. Justnovich for wanting to cut it off.*

*I left early before the serious drinking began. From the Club, the party progressed to the Bachelor Officers' Quarters where 10 young, lovely prostitutes awaited those interested in the pursuit of sensual pleasures.*

The farewell party was not really farewell: I waited over six weeks to receive travel orders. Gene, Marv, and Ron had a similar farewell send-off from the club the previous month. I saw them one last time in Cam Ranh Bay, where they were stationed for the remainder of their tour.

I didn't stay in touch with the officers from my dispensary, but in 1992, I found telephone numbers for all three—and this was pre-Google. I called and invited them to D.C. for a twenty-fifth Vietnam reunion, but no one expressed any interest. Looking back, we all got along, but we were not close friends. We lived and worked together 24/7, but that didn't result in long-term friendships. Regardless, I was saddened that no one wanted to reconnect.

Five years later I called Ron and invited him to Asheville. We caught up on general stuff: jobs, his second marriage and children, and my time in the Army Reserve. Although we were friends, and I shared many adventures with him, I never told him that I was gay and the struggle I was going through that year in Vietnam. That was the last time I talked with him.

In 2012, David Johnson, who had been a dental tech in our unit, called the American Optometric Association and asked for my telephone number. I didn't know David well while we were in Phan Rang. Turns out that he is a fine man. A year or so later, he and his wife visited Tony and me in our home. I value that David and I continue to share experiences and milestones in our lives.

# MILITARY PROTOCOL

***28 May 1967***

*Today I traveled to Cam Ranh Bay via a two-and-one half-ton cargo truck. The trip took longer than usual because the driver didn't know how to shift gears properly, so we never got past third gear all the way to Cam Ranh. Also, a broken-down bus on a single-lane bridge caused us to stop and wait while the Vietnamese passengers unloaded and then pushed the bus over the bridge to the other side of the road. The 101st Airborne driver stood guard with his rifle, but fortunately we were not ambushed.*

*I went to the 61st Battalion Headquarters to discuss obtaining a jeep for Jim and me, taking another R&R and picking up an optical instrument. Results: The instrument I picked up, which was packed 15 years ago and had never been opened, is a useless lamp to illuminate color plates. Marv doesn't care if I take another R&R and advised to forget the jeep request, as Maj. Gold, the Battalion Executive Officer, will never give it up.*

*I also took time to shoot the bull with Marv, Gene, and Ron, whose morale is as low as mine. All three live in the 22nd Replacement area where troops temporarily bunk upon entry and exit of Vietnam. The noise from the carousing troops keeps them from sleeping most nights. They eat in a mess hall that feeds 5,000 troops. They miss the quiet life of Phan Rang.*

*We lamented our woes, and Ron told a couple of stories to lift my spirits. According to Ron, the vacuous Maj. Gold wants "attention" called whenever he or other ranking officers enters a medical facility. After Marv read this directive, he told Ron to never call attention while he was doing a circumcision—he was afraid he might jump or jerk his hands, which could be disastrous for the patient.*

*Recently Gold walked into the dispensary while Marv was performing a circumcision. Ron did not call attention. Gold then turned to Ron and chewed him out. Ron explained that the CO, Capt. Youkilis, had issued an order not to call attention while he was operating.*

*Gold replied, "Couldn't you call attention softly." Ron laughed in his face.*

*Another story Ron told was difficult to believe. Two lieutenants assigned to Military Headquarters in Cam Ranh Bay daily walk around the base taking names of enlisted men who fail to salute. Men caught not saluting must attend a week of special classes in the evenings on military courtesy. This sounds like a scene taken directly from the book,* Catch-22.

I always found it difficult to follow—or sometimes remember—military protocol. For example, was I to walk to the left or right of an officer who outranked me? Don't remember.

Frequently, military protocol represented rigid rules that didn't make sense. When I was in Vietnam, officers and enlisted men in our base camp could not eat together in the same mess tent. You could work, shower, or fight to defend the camp together, but you couldn't eat together.

Protocol was part of the hate in my "love/hate" relationship with the military. Although I didn't have ROTC training, I did learn protocol in Officers' Basic Training, but I pushed back when possible. My motto was, "Rules that don't make sense can be broken." And I did break them.

I never reprimanded anyone for not saluting me. And I

socialized with enlisted corpsmen when I returned to the States even though officers were prohibited from fraternizing because "it could create an actual or predictable adverse impact on discipline, authority, morale, or the ability of the command to accomplish its mission." The army prohibited heterosexual and homosexual relationships between officers and enlisted personnel. But that didn't stop me from dating enlisted men.

After Vietnam, I was assigned to Fort Sill, Oklahoma, which was located near Lawton. Initially, Oklahoma was not OK for me. It was the in the middle of nowhere. No friends. No gay bars. No nothing.

While driving around the main square, I stumbled onto the cruising scene in downtown Lawton, where I met many enlisted soldiers. I fondly remember, Sam, a twenty-three-year-old sergeant assigned to the Cavalry's equestrian detachment. He took care of military horses and rode them in post ceremonies. He was rugged, handsome, and well suited for his job as a military ceremonial soldier. He liked women—and men.

When I met Sam, he was babysitting his ten-month-old baby. Since his wife worked as a waitress, we dated on the nights she worked, and he brought their baby with him. He wanted to remain married, but was looking for a steady boyfriend, and so was I. We dated until he was reassigned to another post.

For several months I dated sweet young Pvt. Danny Boy, who didn't know I was in the military. Although we didn't discuss labels, Danny's interest in me was probably one of situational homosexuality, or perhaps he was bisexual. Coming to my house offered him an escape from the barracks and before he left, he used my phone to call his girlfriend back in Ohio.

Later I became enamored with Spec.4 Dan the Man. I dated him even though we worked at the same hospital. Not smart. (Another hospital corpsman determined I was gay and sent me a dozen roses. Although it was an extravagant gesture, I did not date him.) Dan knew about my multiple violations of military rules. He knew about my liaison with Michele, who was married to a handsome captain on base.

I met Michele when we were cast in the Little Theater's production of *You're a Good Man, Charlie Brown.* She was cast as Lucy, and I played Schroeder. One afternoon I picked her up for play practice. As she got in my car, her little son ran out of the house yelling, "Mommy, why are you going away with Schroeder?" Yes, I had a consensual afternoon tryst in my apartment with Lucy. I was still experimenting. Fifty years later I cringe when I think about my actions that day.

Stupidly, I also told Dan that I had smoked pot with a redhead, straight hospital corpsman. Dan held all the cards: I was a gay, adulterous, pot-smoking officer who socialized with enlisted soldiers. I could be discharged for any of those activities .

How could I, a good Southern boy brought up to shun the evil of homosexuality, adultery, and using drugs, begin indulging in these worldly pleasures? As a man of seventy-five, trying to understand my younger self, I can say this about that (as Richard Nixon said). When the minister—a man of God—told me that he was in love with me, my moral compass switched off and everything was possible. I was not apoplectic about the years of denying my sexuality, but I wanted to make up for lost time. Once I realized that I was gay, I was already condemned, and therefore biblical scriptures had no sway over me.

Dan was not without sin. While I went to Germany for two weeks to visit friends, I left the keys to my apartment and car with him. Upon my return, I was disappointed that Dan didn't meet me at the airport. When I walked into my apartment, I knew the reason.

I found a letter on the kitchen table along with my keys. I cried and cried as I read the letter, which stated that I had done terrible things to him and others so he took some things from my house to make up for my transgressions. (He took my possessions to try to forget about me, right? This makes no sense.) Among the items he took were my sky blue ski jacket, a drum I had bought in Kenya, and a Rod Stewart album. He had requested a transfer and was no longer at Fort Sill. In the letter he threatened to expose my secret life to military officials and my parents if I ever got in touch with him. I believe he panicked during my absence, because he recognized that he cared for me and couldn't handle the reality.

Who could I turn to for advice? I was out of touch with God, so for the first time, I turned to a fortuneteller. A friend recommended a local woman, who was reportedly accurate in her predictions. I dressed in nondescript clothes to avoid giving her clues. I nervously knocked on her door. A modestly dressed middle-aged woman greeted me and invited me into her living room. She used cards for her medium and as she turned them over, she began talking: "You prefer the company of men. You are trying to decide whether to make a trip. The city is near a large body of water. You are very conflicted about visiting a person. You should make the trip. Everything will be all right." My responses were minimal, a head nod, or yes. Without any apparent clues, the fortuneteller helped me decide to confront Dan.

A few months later, I resigned my commission. I was free of military rules and threats. I drove to Washington, D.C., and showed up unannounced at the Pentagon clinic, where Dan worked. I walked into the clinic with confidence because he was still in the military, and I was a civilian.

When he saw me, his ashen face confirmed that I now held the cards. He asked his supervisor for the afternoon off, and we drove back to his apartment. After talking for over an hour, I knew that he did care for me, but he was not ready to renew our relationship.

He said, "Let's think about all this and talk again." When I left his apartment, I felt that a piece of my heart had been torn out. I returned to my car, broke down, and sobbed uncontrollably.

He never called me, nor did he return any of my personal items. Of all my past relationships, Dan remains unfinished business.

# BANGKOK

***30 May 1967***

*Today I flew to Bangkok for five days of R & R. The Pan Am flight took less than three hours. Upon landing in Bangkok, I located a special bus heading to an R & R briefing at Tommie's Tourist Agency. Tommie's caters to American servicemen and with 6,000 troops arriving monthly, this is quite an operation, employing about 50 men and women as guides and drivers. After the Army Captain in charge of R & R briefed us on Thai customs, Tommie Tourist girls held us captive while they sold tours. I bought a shopping, floating market, and a Tim Land tour.*

*I chose the Century Hotel, which seemed nice from the photos, with air-conditioned rooms and a pool. A few minutes after arriving in my hotel room, a Danny's Car Service representative invaded my room to sell me a rental car and driver for five days. He started at $30 and wouldn't go below $25 for all five days. Rather than trying to find a taxi and getting lost and not speaking the language, I agreed to the deal. I realized I needed a cab because the city is spread out with no central business area. I soon learned that the taxi drivers have a racket whereby they receive a percentage of the price you pay for anything you buy at various shops. As a result the shopkeeper marks up the price so the cabbie can have some of the* *profit.*

*After dinner tonight, my driver picked me up in his 1956 beat-up Chevy. He took me to The Swinger, which was packed with American GIs and bar girls. The band played bad versions of American rock-and-roll while two Thai girls tried to sing. The place was almost totally dark when suddenly the lights came on the dance floor, the music grew louder and about 20 bar girls flooded the dance area, each with a number on her dress.*

*The game is "pick a number for the night," pay the cashier $11, receive a paid receipt, and the young lovely is yours. The whole thing was disgusting to me. It was like a cattle auction or supermarket where you pick a cut of meat. Ugh! I left early.*

Here is what I didn't record in my journal, but really happened at the club:

I selected one of the comely, numbered girls and paid for an expensive soda. (I should have asked for a magical elixir to help overcome my inhibition and nervousness.) I didn't know her age, but I would guess about eighteen—maybe younger or older. After small talk, I asked her if I could take her out of the club. That is when she told me about the payment with the bar cashier. I could pay extra, and she could spend the night with me. I went to the cashier, paid the full fee, and got a receipt.

She was not in a hurry to go to my hotel. Instead, we walked to her friend's house, which was built on stilts over the water. She asked me to remove my shoes outside the door. The house was well kept, furnished sparsely, and revealed shiny clean floors. I remember the feature of the main room—a large picture of the young king of Thailand. In retrospect, the house visit was the highlight of the evening.

We went back to my hotel room, lay on the bed, and I planted a perfunctory kiss on her cheek. No sparks from either of us. I touched her hair and she said, "No." I don't know if it was a cultural issue or she didn't want me to muss her hair. Perhaps touching was mutually difficult.

Whether it was her objection to touching her hair or my guilt for sleeping with a prostitute, my heterosexual experiment with this girl was over, and I asked her to leave. She said, "Okay, but give me the receipt from the cashier. I must return it in order to be paid."

I bellowed in rage, "No." She began crying and pleading for me to give her the receipt.

I yelled, "Get out," as I angrily threw the receipt on the bed. She took it and left.

I am not proud of this scene and have not shared the story until now. I cannot justify my action with this girl any more than I can with the other women I led on. After failing previously, I was again experimenting, searching for sexual feelings for a woman. What was wrong with me? I was young and was trying to conform to the expectations of the military and my family. Again and again.

***31 May 1967***

*I began the day with a hot bath, my first since R & R in Hong Kong. After breakfast my driver took me on a tour of temples on the palace grounds of King Bhumibol Adulyadej and Queen Sirikit. I sensed pride and respect by the Thai people for the royal couple and noted that shopkeepers displayed their pictures. I was told that the king and queen leave for a U.S. tour in two weeks.*

*The steeply peaked roofs and towers reminded me of a fairy tale setting. Or maybe a movie set for The King and I. The Emerald Buddha Temple houses the Buddha, which is made of semi-precious green stone and clothed in gold. I was impressed that people were using the temple during lunchtime to worship and talk with friends, while sitting in a yoga position with their bare feet tucked under their legs. At the entrance of the temple people were placing flowers and burning incense to an image of Buddha.*

*After returning to the hotel for lunch at poolside, I went on a shopping trip. The driver took me to three stores selling bronze flatware, Thai silk, carvings, and jewelry. The Volkswagen bus we rode was supplied by one of the jewelry stores on our itinerary, so I'm sure there was a kickback. You can't beat the syndicate.*

*Regarding the syndicate, I stood firm with my driver tonight when I told him that I wanted to eat at the Baan Thai restaurant. He said, "I know a better place." I replied, "No, I want to go there." And just as advertised, "The Baan Thai Restaurant offered a delicious genuine Thai food in the traditional Thai manner, served by charming ladies dressed in their attractive national costumes." The five dishes were all served at one time: beef with peppers, sweet and sour shrimp, stuffed fried eggplant, chicken curry, and beef soup with potatoes shaped like birds. A large wooden bowl of rice was served with the dishes. I learned to eat the food with a spoon and fork using the fork to push the food into the spoon. Fresh tropical fruit was served for dessert.*

*While sipping hot tea I watched Thai classical dancing, which reminded me of ballet with the addition of intricate hand movements. The hostess, who spoke in English, introduced the dancers wearing colorful, glittering costumes. Across from me were eight Frenchmen, and I'm sure other nationalities were in the room. I guess English is becoming the international language.*

*After dinner I went to Caesar's Palace, located on the seventh floor of the BOA building. The doorman greeted me dressed as a Roman soldier complete with armor and skirt reaching just above his knees. Inside the club, waitresses wore mini togas and one woman wore a Cleopatra-type flowing white garment, which was open in the front down from the waist to the floor.*

*I was sitting at the bar enjoying the English-singing band, when Arlene began talking to me. Arlene, who works at the bar to entertain lonely customers, informed me that I didn't have to pay the bar to take out a girl. Meanwhile, a dirty old man was pawing at her from the opposite side of the barstool. I left.*

Yes, I did leave Caesar's Palace alone. Arlene, who appeared to be an experienced older woman, did not tempt me. It was not "*Groundhog Day*," after all.

***1 June 1967***

*I awoke to the sound of hillbilly music on the hotel's music system. Apparently the Thais think that all Americans enjoy country music.*

*I got up early because the tour of the floating market began at 0700. The traffic at this hour is as wild as any other time. Not only do they drive on the wrong side of the road, but the worst part is that no one seems to have the right-of-way at intersections. The streets are pure madness as cars race along at 45 M.P.H. or faster.*

*On the way to the canal we passed hundreds of school children dressed in their various private school uniforms. If Thai children are fortunate enough to attend private school, they begin studying English in the second grade. I was told there is no public school system, thus poor children may never go to school.*

*The busy canal was filled with as many tourists as indigenous traders. The boy steering our boat had to shove other boats aside to progress through the narrow channel. Our guide bought us bananas from one of the sampan floating stores. Other sampans were loaded with charcoal, fresh meat, vegetables and fruit.*

*At one floating market shopping center I saw a familiar face. Dr. Tom Hannum, the civilian M.D. from Utah, who was my patient in Phan Rang, was on his way back to the U.S. via Bangkok and Bombay, India. Small world.*

*Along the canal the houses are built on stilts over the water, where children were swimming in their "front yards." Many of the houses were shacks with rusted tin roofs. Freshly washed clothes hung from lines. Potted plants provided a green, lush contrast to the murky, gray water below.*

*Further up the canal we stopped at the Wat Arun or Temple of the Dawn. Constructed in the 17th Century and located on the bank of the Chao Phraya River, the tall grey stone pagoda structure has steps up to the top. I had a phenomenal bird's-eye view of the canal and the buildings across the river.*

*After lunch I went to Bangkok Jewelry where I bought bronze flatware, silk and a set of jade earrings. I bargained the clerk for the bronze flatware down from $45 to $38 for service for 12—including fish knives.*

*I was tired after three hours of shopping and asked Danny to take me for a steam bath and massage. He took me to—believe it or not—Happy, Happy Ltd. Inside the lobby were GIs sitting and talking with girls. One wall of the room was a gigantic two-way mirror, which revealed a dozen girls waiting to be selected by a number pinned to their dress.*

*The mama-san in charge of the female workers and my driver advised me to pick number 32, because she spoke good English. I asked, "Don't they all speak good English?"*

*She replied, "Oh, yes."*

*I picked a pretty girl, number 14. When we went to our massage room, I learned that her English consisted of about 10 words or less. In an effort to appear professional, she wore a white jacket over her bathing suit. There was no steam bath—just a hot bath and massage for five dollars. She implied that I could have more by paying more. I didn't.*

I could have asked my driver to take me to a bath for a legitimate massage, as I did in Hong Kong. But I was still working on being normal by seeking out a girl massage. The result: an unremarkable massage.

It was an astonishing coincidence that I saw Tom Hannum in Bangkok. Small world, indeed. After talking to him about his circuitous route returning to the U.S. through India, I decided to request the same route home at the end of my tour.

***2 June 1967***

*Today I went to TIM Land (Thailand in Miniature), a theme park—Disneyland without the rides. The park was designed to provide a taste of all of Thailand's culture in one place. In the first building I saw demonstrations of clay pot and silk making. Walking out of the crafts building, I saw young men leading two elephants to work. The men shouted a command and the elephants pulled and pushed logs into a stream.*

*In an outdoor covered theater, I saw folk dancing accompanied by girls playing bamboo instruments. Next came two men showing us Thai boxing techniques. The boxing reminded me of American professional wrestling with fake groans and showmanship. The men used their fists, elbows, knees, feet or any part of their body to fight.*

*Cock fighting, which was appalling, was the next event. Less engaging was an aquarium of dazzling red Siamese fighting fish. Keeping with the fighting theme, two young boys fought with sticks about five feet long, and it amazed me that the boys didn't get hurt. They put on an excellent show, as did the men sword fighting, which caused sparks to fly from the clashing of steel blades.*

*My guide to Tim Land was Aura, an 18-year-old attractive Thai girl who spoke fluent English. I asked her out to dinner tonight, but she explained, "Good girls are looked down on for going out with American GIs." Since she lives with her mother, she follows her advice—no Americans. Aura had plans to join her brother studying in San Francisco, but when her father died two months ago, she decided to stay with her mother for the time being.*

***3 June 1967***

*Although Aura turned down my dinner invitation (the escargot dish was outstanding), this morning she called to invite me to Pattaya Bang Beach, about 70 miles southeast from Bangkok. The $8 tour from Tommie's Tourist was free, because I was Aura's guest.*

*I saw mostly Americans at the beach, which featured water skiing and horseback riding. Aura and I chose horseback riding, which proved to be a painful experience. We returned to the beach where I met a dentist stationed at Long Benh, and we went to lunch with several Thai people including Aura. The beach trip turned into a full day of adventure.*

*I ate dinner tonight alone at the Monohra Hotel in the Botany Room. The restaurant was dark, dead, and morbid. Or the room simply reflected my mood, because tomorrow I am leaving Bangkok to return to the Nam. The room featured tropical plants and palms—perhaps 10 feet tall. I was sitting next to one of the giant palms, while a mouse (not Mickey) played around in the greenery. When I told the waiter what I witnessed, he only smiled. In spite of the mouse escapade, I finished my meal.*

From the touristy TIM Land shows to the floating market, the trip to Bangkok was captivating. The bar and message establishment

I experienced was tame compared to the notorious nightlife that is currently available. I have seen photos of Bangkok ladyboys* depicted in Las Vegas-style shows and go-go bars. If ladyboy shows were available, my resourceful driver would have informed me.

Thirty-seven years later, I visited my old friend, Ben, and experienced up close and personal the acceptance of a Thai transgender woman into society. Ben, who lives in Den Haag, in Holland, had a Thai boyfriend for many years, but I had never met Somsak.

As I sat in the lobby of my Amsterdam hotel, I noticed an attractive Asian woman walking with Ben. He introduced me to Salina, who excused herself to go to the restroom. Ben read the confusion on my face and explained. Five years ago, Somsak told Ben that he wanted to transition. Ben didn't sign up for this, but accepted the change. Formerly, they were legally married as husband and husband and now as husband and wife. He said they were happy and told me about a recent return trip to Salina's hometown, where she visited family and friends with complete acceptance.

My visit with Ben and Salina occurred a decade earlier than the passage of North Carolina's infamous HB2, which forced transgender people to use bathrooms based on their biological sex as stated on their birth certificate. In 2017, HB2 was overturned, but the compromise HB 142 left in place restrictions for local government to expand protections for gay and transgender people.

It took North Carolina fifteen years to catch up with Holland's law that legalized marriage between same-sex couples. Will it take another fifteen to grant equal rights for transgender people? I hope not.

---

* Ladyboy is a common term in Thailand and refers to a gay effeminate male or transgender person, who generally works in the entertainment or sex business. The politically correct term is transgender woman.

# WALLS

***5 June 1967***

*The world is in chaos. For several weeks there have been demonstrations and riots in Hong Kong by communists sympathetic to Red China. Demonstrations against the Vietnam War have been occurring in San Francisco, Washington, DC, and New York. Police clashed with over 10,000 protestors in Los Angles, where President Johnson was speaking. There were also race riots in Detroit and Newark.*

*To add to the world's unrest, Israel declared war today on its Arab neighbors.*

***11 June 1967***

*The Middle East war lasted just six days with little Israel triumphing over all the Arab nations. Gene Fishman said, "Israel has done it again." Indeed. Perhaps the U.S. could learn something from Israel on how to win a war in six days.*

Israel initiated the war against Syria, Jordan, and Egypt to prevent what they perceived as an impending attack by their neighbors. The war was an implausible win for Israel as they captured the West Bank of the Jordan River, the Sinai, the Golan Heights, and

Jerusalem. The Six Day War was the third Arab-Israeli war since the creation of the state of Israel, but not the last of the fighting, which continues today—fifty years later. Several generations of Palestinians have lived under Israel occupation.

In 1970, I traveled in the Middle East to Lebanon, Egypt, Cyprus, and Israel. In Cairo, I was amazed to find armed guards on the bridges and in front of large buildings. At night, cab drivers drove with their headlights off until we came to an intersection. I sensed that the government anticipated war and was creating an atmosphere of fear among its people. In the Egyptian Antiquities Museum, there were sandbags around the ancient artifacts—including objects from the tomb of Tutankhamun. Ironically, the sandbags were stamped *USAID* with a logo of a handshake.

Israel prohibited direct flights from Egypt (their declared enemy) so I arranged a stopover in Cyprus before continuing on to Tel Aviv. Arriving in Israel, I immediately noticed a refreshing difference from Egypt. In the brilliant sun I saw smiling young people and smelled the redolent orange blossoms. I visited a kibbutz where young boys and girls from Africa, Russian and Eastern Europe seemed optimistic and joyful. Maybe this was the Promised Land. I fell in love with Israel.

I visited the Church of the Nativity and the Mount of Olives, where Jesus walked in days of long ago. At the muddy Jordan River, I remembered Bible story and old gospel hymns.

Nine years later, I was in Washington, D.C., when President Jimmy Carter oversaw the Camp David negotiations, which resulted in the peace treaty between Egypt and Israel. Presidents since Carter have tried without success to resolve the continuing Arab-Israeli dispute via a two-state solution. Many U.S. legislators remain beholden to the powerful Israeli lobbyists in Washington.

According to the American-Israeli Cooperative Enterprise, in 2017 there were 420,899 Jewish people living in settlements on the West Bank. In retaliation, Palestinians have launched thousands of rockets at Israel from Gaza. And Israel responds by destroying the homes of the perpetrators and their families. My heart goes out to the Palestinian children, who continue to pay the price of war created by adults. The chaos from Israel's occupation of Arab land continues.

In the guise of security, Israel has built a four hundred mile long barrier. It consists of eight-foot-tall concrete walls in urban areas and layers of pyramid-shaped barbed wire fencing in other areas.

Building a wall to separate populations is not unique. Russia built a wall to separate Communist East Berlin from West Berlin. In 1971, I witnessed the hideous wall up close at Checkpoint Charlie. With my military ID card in hand, I walked the barren street, spanning about a long city block, from West Berlin to communist East Berlin. The five-minute walk was eerie and sobering, as was the sight of East Berlin looming ahead. I held my ID card in front of the border guard and continued to walk without speaking. The people I saw on the street were a reflection of the gray, somber, concrete buildings, which were constructed by Russia after the war. I bought a few hand-carved Christmas ornaments from a joyless shopkeeper and hurriedly returned to West Berlin.

In 1987, President Ronald Reagan, the Hollywood actor and icon of Republican conservatives, went to West Berlin and said to the Russian leader:

> "Behind me stands a wall that encircles the free sectors of this city, part of a vast system of barriers that divides the entire continent of Europe. . . . Standing before the Brandenburg Gate, every man is a German, separated from his fellow men. Every man is a Berliner, forced to look upon a scar.... Mr. Gorbachev, tear down this wall!"

Reagan's powerful words are as true then as they are today. But Republicans haven't followed in Reagan's footsteps. In 2006, President George W. Bush signed a bill that constructed 698 miles of fence along the U.S.-Mexican border. Donald Trump, the reality TV star-turned-president, has compounded upon the sentiment, promising to build a thousand-mile impenetrable concrete wall and, absurdly, force the Mexican government to pay for it.

In 2009, when I returned to Berlin, I could find only a few panels remained to remind me of the wall's dark chapter of history. At Checkpoint Charlie, tourists were posing with an actor dressed in U.S. Army uniform. People were laughing and having fun. There was no wall separating free people.

Perhaps someday Israel will take down its fence. And maybe the U.S. will, as well. I hold on to hope. Look at Berlin.

Almost ten years after I told my parents I was gay, it was evident that my mother and I still had a wall—invisible but real—between us. It was obvious in conversations. Perhaps out of fear of the AIDS epidemic, my mother asked me if I was still dating men. It was not a pleasant conversation because her questions held a judgmental tone. In so many words, I made it clear that I was gay and could never change. The conversation ended when my mother stated, "As long as there is life, there is hope."

When my mother stated her hope, it was not in reference to the Berlin Wall coming down. Oh, no. She was expressing hope to live to see me become heterosexual. As much as I loved my mother and wanted to please her, I couldn't become what she wanted. I believe what the Apostle Paul said, "But whatever I am now, it is all because God poured out his special favor on me..."

In spite of the pronouncement that she was hoping for my change, my mother and I had a good relationship over the years. I continued to visit my parents and took them on yearly vacations. When my mother was confined to a wheelchair, I took her to shop for clothes, shoes, and facial products. We could talk about most anything, and she continued to surprise me (in a good way) with her observations.

Over my lifetime, I have worked at taking down walls I created out of fear of losing my military career, my family, and the love of God. With my parents, I accepted that their unreal expectations would never change, but we could love each other grounded in deep mutual respect.

In a recent conversation with a dear friend, Nancie McDermott, I was made aware of a wall of separation I had created between two mutual friends and myself. I was hurt by the separation, but I had done nothing to try to restore our relationship. Nancie encouraged me to contact them. "Don't try to justify past actions. Move forward." Good advice for Israel, Palestine, and me.

# JIMMY, I HARDLY KNEW YOU

***19 June 1967***

*Jim Mahoney—and his gigantic walrus mustache—left for Cam Ranh today to wait for his DEROS (date eligible for return from overseas). I now have the Hex house to myself. Neither his replacement nor mine has arrived yet. Typical army planning.*

*Each night after dinner Jim went to his dental office and began drinking, while writing a letter to his wife and two young sons. The letters were long, and written in beautiful cursive calligraphy. Afterwards, depending on his mood, he frequently drove to the club to continue his drinking.*

*Jim had a quick, acerbic wit, and he liked to pull practical jokes. Sometimes he did crazy things while drunk. He told me last week that he had been kicked out of the Australian Enlisted Men's Club for pissing on the bar. Another night at the Officers' Club he had "borrowed" a jeep from the parking lot without anyone's consent. He vaguely remembered other details of that evening.*

*Earlier this week, around 2100 hours, I found him passed out in the dental clinic with his head on his desk. I was going to let him stay there until he woke up, but about an hour later a corpsman woke me up and asked, "Are you going to let Capt. Mahoney spend the night at his desk?"*

*The answer was, of course, "No." Together we carried Jim to his bed.*

*His latest fun game is calling up various drinking partners the morning after to find out what he did the previous night. Great sport!*

*In spite of his late-night drinking, he somehow got up every day and saw patients. And I didn't hear any complaints about his dental work.*

Several months after I returned to the States, during the time I was stationed at Fort Bragg, I got a late-night call from Ron and Jim. I don't remember the specifics of the conversation. Basically it was a "How's it going?" and "What's new?" type of call. I was pleased to hear from them.

The following June, Ron called me again. Jim had committed suicide on Mother's Day, 1968—less than a year after returning from Vietnam. He hanged himself in the basement of his house, leaving behind his wife and two young sons. I think he was thirty-one years old. Ron didn't know any details or if there was a suicide note. Was it a crazy prank that went wrong? What were his issues that caused him to kill himself...on Mother's Day? I don't have a clue.

The shocking news disquieted me. I shared a tent and three meals a day with this man for a year, and I hardly knew him. And to be fair, he knew nothing about my mental battles with religion and sexual orientation.

I credit my survival to gradually transmuting my sense of separation, enabling me again to talk to God—asking, thanking, and acknowledging his presence in my daily life.

Why should I be separated from my Creator? No religion can tell me that God doesn't love and accept me: God *is* love. I am not always the person I could be, but I ask God for help to be a better person.

# CIRCUITOUS EXIT

***1 July 1967***

*Today I received a call from the 43rd Medical Group Personnel Office telling me to come to Cam Ranh Bay to pick up my orders. In a last-minute scramble, I packed my military footlocker with a few personal items, along with the cache of war: peasant shirt and pants, spears from the Montagnard, and a defused hand grenade.*

*I saw patients this morning, which made my last day even more hectic, and left the 101st base camp hurriedly, without goodbyes and without a replacement optometrist. I had planned to shake hands with everyone and wish them well, but time ran out. I hitched a ride to the air terminal in order to take the last flight of the day out of Phan Rang.*

*I arrived in Cam Ranh to learn that Ron and Marv had left country earlier, and only Gene and I remained from our original dispensary officer staff.*

*I found Gene in the Officers' Club killing time. As usual he had some stories to tell. Several weeks ago a famous TV star was touring Vietnam with the musical Guys and Dolls, which played at a convalescent center near the dispensary. The star asked to see a physician about his hemorrhoid condition and was taken to Gene. When Gene asked him to describe his problem, he whipped out his penis. It was a typical story about a party in Nha Trang with local, lovely beauties and drinking too much. Later he had symptoms indicating gonorrhea and was given tetracycline tablets. He wanted to make sure everything was O.K. down there.*

*Tomorrow Gene and I will be clearing post—obtaining official release from 43rd Medical Group.*

***4 July 1967***

*I wanted to spend Independence Day somewhere other than in Vietnam. No such luck. But I was able to pick up my circuitous travel orders:*

> *HEADQUARTERS 43rd MEDICAL GROUP*
> *SPECIAL ORDERS Number 166*
> *Pert to: WHITENER, JOHNNY C, CPT MSC,*
> *221st Med Det APO 96377*
> *Special Instructions: Report to Tri Svc ATCO TSN NLT 1045*
> *on 6 July 67*
> *Dept 6 July 67*
> *Flt No: 561*
> *Dept Time: 1345*
> *Countries to be visited: Japan, Thailand, India, Afghanistan, Greece, Italy, England, France and Austria.*

*My plan was to fly to India then to Europe—Italy, France or England—and then to New York. With my orders approved I was able to book a seat on the U.S. Embassy flight from Saigon to New Delhi.*

***5 July 1967***

*After waiting in Cam Ranh Bay for several days, Gene and I left for Saigon today. We landed at 8th Aerial Port and waited for a military bus to go to the civilian air terminal. (For security reasons, Vietnamese taxi cabs can't go to the Aerial Port.) At Tan Son Nhut terminal I checked into the Tri Service ATCO desk to verify my flight to India tomorrow. My flight was confirmed and I was assured that all was in order.*

*Gene, another officer, and myself, along with out luggage, managed to squeeze into a pint-sized Renault taxi. The car was so crowded that the driver had difficulty shifting gears. On the way to our hotel, he calmly vied for space with pedicabs, bicycles and pedestrians. A wild ride.*

*Gene and I stayed at the King's Palace—hardly a palace—but the room was air-conditioned. I had dinner at the Brink (a military BOQ building) and retired early to sleep.*

***6 July 1967***

*We left the Palace about 0930 for the air terminal, which was only seven kilometers from the hotel. After driving around in circles, it was clear that the driver was lost. We got out of his car and found a military bus, which took us to the airport. I said goodbye to Gene, who was flying to Tokyo.*

*Around 1115 hours I heard an announcement that all passengers on the manifest of Flight 561 to New Delhi, India, should report to the check-in counter. After looking through my passport, Capt. Harrison asked for my visa to India. I didn't have a visa stamp for India because no one told me it was necessary. He said, "You must have the visa stamp or you can't board the plane." Another officer was in the same predicament.*

*I couldn't believe it. After all the trouble I went through to obtain the proper orders and had obtained a confirmed seat on the Embassy flight to New Delhi, a captain—my age and rank—was denying my departure from Vietnam. I asked, "How can I get a visa?"*

*"You can go to the American Embassy, but you don't have time," he said.*

*"I will go to the Embassy and return with the visa. Hold my luggage until I return with the visa." He agreed.*

*We had one-and-a-half hours before the flight took off. According to Capt. Harrison, this was mission impossible! We walked several blocks to get a taxi and waved enough piasters in his face so that he agreed to take us to the Embassy at breakneck speed. The traffic was stop and go. Mostly stop.*

*When we arrived at the American Embassy, the staff was leaving for lunch. We stopped three men, who looked official, and told them about needing a visa. One of the men said, "We can't help you because you need to go to the Indian Embassy." Swell. They agreed to drop us there on their way to a restaurant.*

*Inside the Indian Embassy we learned that the Consulate General was at lunch. The little Indian man at the desk could care less if we ever visited his country. After hurriedly spilling our story he said, "You need three photographs and return in two hours after lunch." Again we pleaded our case and told him we didn't have time to return after lunch. Then he changed his story. "You don't have to have a visa to visit India this year because it is International Tourist Year." He typed a statement attesting to this fact and stamped it with the Consulate General's stamp.*

*Finding a cab in downtown Saigon during lunch is nearly impossible, but we were successful. We arrived at the air terminal from our completely unnecessary trip to two embassies with twenty minutes remaining before departure of our flight. Passengers for the flight were beginning to board as we rushed up to the desk and presented Capt. Harrison with the officially stamped paper from the Indian Embassy.*

*"You're too late," he said with a smirk. "I've given your seats away." The jerk gave our seats away while holding our luggage for our return from the wild goose chase for a needless visa. "Remove the passenger who has my seat," I requested. He refused. I asked to speak to his commanding officer, but he said, "He is in Bangkok on temporary duty."*

*I went ballistic. In a booming voice full of righteous indignation, I told him that I would ask my congressman, Rep. Basil Whitener, for an investigation. I asked, and he gave me his complete name and unit address.*

*Since the next flight to India was in seven days, and all seats were filled, we had to change our plans. The officer who had accompanied me on our visa adventure requested the next flight to the States. I requested the next flight to Japan, which was permitted with my travel orders. I couldn't get a confirmed seat and was placed on standby status.*

*For the next twenty-six hours I waited for a flight out of Saigon. I tried to sleep and eat in the filthy, mosquito-infested hole, but with little success. The terminal's Vietnamese-operated restaurant was swarming with flies, which didn't seem to mind the high prices. I had soup, bread and hot tea, which I hoped were safe for consumption.*

Rep. Basil Whitener (no relation) was a congressman from North Carolina. After returning to the States, I wrote him detailing the incident with Capt. Harrison. Months later I received a response, which in essence absolved the captain from all wrongdoing.

To this day I am irritated when I remember how Capt. Harrison misused his power—rather than using his brain—to deny me the flight to India. Passengers were still boarding the plane; he could have given me my seat.

Years later I was returning from business in D.C. to Asheville on a flight through Charlotte. It was a busy Friday afternoon, which meant the plane departed late from D.C., and everyone wanted to get home for the weekend. On the same flight was U.S. Congressman Heath Shuler, who was trying to catch the Asheville plane as well. Upon touchdown in Charlotte, we both made a galloping dash to catch the flight to Asheville. When we arrived at the gate, the plane had not pushed off, but the door was closed. I asked the clerk if we could board. She refused. Flashback to Capt. Harrison, who is now a woman in a U.S. Airlines uniform. I shouted and raved, but it made no difference. Rep. Shuler didn't say a word. He had learned, as I should have, that airline personnel have absolute power. And they know it.

***7 July 1967***

*At 1430 today I left Vietnam on a C-141, the military jet cargo plane. Farewell, Vietnam, forever.*

*The uncomfortable seats were made of canvas straps, which folded against the side of the plane when not used. The other three passengers and I shared the flight with pallets of cargo. The Pfc.*

*sitting next to me was returning to the States so his wife could divorce him. How awful.*

*The cargo flight offered no food or heat. Well into our flight, a crewmember came from the cockpit and offered us blankets to help keep warm and returned to the cockpit, leaving us on our own. I wrapped myself in a blanket and was still cold.*

*The plane stopped at Clark Air Base, Philippines to refuel and to change cargo.* We had a chance to get off the freezing plane to warm up and eat in an American-style restaurant.*

I am trying to recapture my feelings as I left Vietnam. I hated the dirt sticking to my face, breathing the soupy heat, sleeping under mosquito netting and wearing Army fatigues each day. I simply wanted to get out. I arrived in Vietnam with an insular view of the world and left challenged by books and travel that opened my mind to new experiences and caused me to question my values. I credit my tour of duty as changing my life forever. While I fondly remember the fantastic tangerine-colored sunsets, I have no interest in returning to visit Vietnam because neither the country nor I are the same.

***8 July 1967***

*I arrived in Tachikawa, Japan at 0630—14 hours after leaving Saigon. I haven't shaved or bathed in three days.*

*I decided to take a train from the airport to the center of Tokyo. While I was standing on the platform looking confused, a Japanese man came up to me and offered to help me find the correct train. The train was crowed because it was morning rush hour, but I managed to stand with two cameras hanging around my neck and holding on to one suitcase for the entire 50-minute ride.*

*I found the Hotel Akahoma, which is a fusion of a Japanese and western hotel. The furniture, however—including the bed—was designed for shorter Japanese clients. Instead of a western-style terry-cloth bathrobe, I tried on the lightweight, cotton, blue*

* Clark was vital to logistical support for the Vietnam War.

*and white Japanese kimono in the closet. I liked it and bought it.*

*I slept for a few hours and walked around Tokyo. I discovered a restaurant with beautiful plates of food with prices displayed in the window. Since the menus were in Japanese only, I pointed to the dish I wanted. I was shocked when the waiter brought me a plate of raw hamburger and bread. Since I was not up to a gastronomic adventure, I asked for the meat to be cooked. To my chagrin, I later learned about steak tartare.*

*I found a movie theater showing* The Taming of the Shrew *with Elizabeth Taylor and Richard Burton. The movie was dubbed into Japanese with English subtitles. What would Shakespeare think?*

Later I learned that the window display of steak tartare and other dishes were made of plastic. The menu items were painted with convincing details—food art. Amazing.

***9 July***

*I went to a Baptist church service this morning. Afterwards I bought an umbrella and walked around in the rain. Even in the misty rain, Mount Fuji majestically loomed in the distance.*

*As I paused at a corner looking lost, a man stopped in his car to ask if he could help me with directions. This is the second time a friendly stranger has offered to help me in the big city of Tokyo.*

My friendly encounters occurred only twenty years after Americans bombed and killed thousands of people while destroying Hiroshima and Nagasaki. The friendliness of the Japanese toward Americans continues. My brother Ron was there in 2015 and remarked to me how friendly people were. Even drivers were courteous.

I suppose it is cultural, and I like it.

***11 July 1967***

*Before I left Phan Rang, I told a Red Cross worker that I might travel to Japan on my way to the States. She gave me the name and contact information for a Japanese friend. I called Setsuko and we met in a French restaurant near my hotel. She was pleasant and formal. She teaches history in a girl's school but wants a new job as a simultaneous interpreter.*

*After lunch, we took the subway to a tranquil traditional Japanese garden. The subway station was impressive with lovely mosaic tile walls and modern shops. Since Setsuko had an evening Japanese-English class, we parted and agreed to meet tomorrow evening.*

*In the evening, I watched the newly released movie,* You Only Live Twice. *James Bond speaking Japanese was weird. But Nancy Sinatra's theme song was in English.*

***12 July 1967***

*This morning I took a short train ride to Yokohama City. Yokohama, a seaport town. I had a seafood lunch in a Chinese restaurant.*

*I returned to Tokyo in time to meet Setsuko at the Imperial Theatre for the original stage play of* Gone with the Wind *in Japanese. Fortunately, I rented a transistor device that simultaneously translated the dialogue into English. (By mere coincidence Vivian Leigh, the original Scarlett O'Hara, died four days ago. Until now, no one has tried to re-create her role or stage* Gone with the Wind *since the original movie.)*

*The production began at 1730 and ran until 2200 with two intermissions—yes, almost five hours. And this was only part two of the Margaret Mitchell classic! Part one previously ran for five months. The forty minutes of intermission allowed time for eating dinner while standing in the lobby.*

*The play begins four years into the Civil War with a live orchestra overture, film clips, and narration to summarize the previous events. Scarlett, played by actress Wataru Nachi, was pretty with her long curly hair and gorgeous costumes. Akira Takarada was the Asian-looking Rhett Butler. The sight of Japanese southern gentlemen in red and blond wigs, and the servants and mammies in blackface with banjos playing in the background, was amusing. The fighting scenes were overacted by exaggerated swinging of their arms.*

*There were at least ten elaborate, revolving sets. The most impressive scene depicted Scarlett in a buggy pulled across stage by a live horse while shacks in a sawmill town were burning, the stage filled with smoke and (with realistic special effects) buildings disintegrating in flames.*

*After the show I took Setsuko home, which turned out to be as fascinating as the play I had just witnessed. She lives with her mother in a striking, simple, traditional-style Japanese house in a quiet residential area. At the door I was asked to take off my shoes, and her mother offered me tiny white cloth house shoes. Setsuko giggled as I wiggled my size twelve feet into the tiny slippers. Her mother, who was wearing a beautiful kimono, excused herself and disappeared behind a sliding shoji rice paper door. She returned with a tray of glasses and Coca-Cola. I suppose she thought all Americans like Coke, but I would have preferred tea. Visiting Setsuko's home was a treat.*

It was a fun, cultural mind-blowing experience to see the Japanese production of *Gone with the Wind*! In 1972, a musical version was staged in London, a French musical production in 2006, and a Broadway musical adapted by Sir Trevor Nunn in 2008. The Broadway version received negative reviews and closed after two months. Outlasting the Broadway version, the Japanese version, which I saw, played for three months.

After five days of hearing only Japanese on the streets, seeing two American movies with subtitles, and a play in Japanese, I was ready to hear English. It was time to go home and face the "thorn in my flesh."

# BOYFRIENDS

On July 12, 1967, my army tour in Southeast Asia ended, as did my journal entries. I was weary of writing in my journal and wanted to get back to the States and experience life—not record it.

All the men in our dispensary at Phan Rang returned home safely after their Vietnam tour. We were among the lucky guys. Of course, this was not true for 58,220 U.S. Soldiers who were killed in action, in accidents, and from complications from wounds, as well as those who died from homicide, self-inflicted wounds, and illness. The numbers don't include soldiers' future morbidity from Agent Orange*, suicide, alcohol and drug addiction, or head trauma and other wounds.

When I chose to leave Vietnam via Japan, I gave up all my plans to travel to India and Europe. (The army would send me there one year later.) I don't recall specific details about the military plane from Tokyo to Travis Air Force Base, California , or whether we stopped in the Philippines, Wake Island, or Honolulu to refuel. The flight was arduous but uneventful.

Travis Air Force Base was only about fifty miles from San

---

*Agent Orange was a chemical herbicide sprayed to kill foliage. Soldiers have suffered from cancer and other medical problems resulting from exposure.

Francisco. I didn't go into the city because I had no idea it was a gay mecca. Instead I caught a commercial airline and flew to Chicago to see an old girlfriend, whose name I can't remember. How could I forget her name? Because she was but one of a number of women I dated in my failed effort to be "normal." Effort is the key word; it didn't come naturally for me.

During my year in Vietnam, I had dated three women and paid for the company of two other women. While I desired men, I neither dated nor had an intimate relationship with a man. But my dating pattern would change during my next military assignment.

I requested a European tour, but instead I was sent to Fort Bragg, North Carolina. For privacy, I found a duplex house in Fayetteville—ten miles from Fort Bragg. Away from military housing and prying eyes, I could date men, bring them to my apartment and continue the compartmentalization of my life.

I continued dating women publicly at official military social events to deflect potential rumors. And for a time, I dated tall, blonde Claudia, whom I met at Fayetteville Baptist Church. My memories of her have faded, but I remember that I brought her to my parents' home for a weekend. I think the highlight for her was driving the tractor with Daddy. Daddy liked her more than I did.

In the year after I returned from Vietnam, two events occurred that helped me confront the reality of being gay. First was the married minister and father of three children who professed his love for me shortly after I returned from Vietnam.

Second, I met Gilberto in Rio.

A clinic patient told me about free military flights from Charleston Airbase, South Carolina, to Rio de Janeiro. I was intrigued and, with military leave papers in hand, drove to Charleston and waited for a space-available seat on a cargo plane. The long flight to Rio was broken up with a stop-over in Surinam, where I stayed in a beautiful hotel built on the side of a mountain. The next morning I continued the flight to Rio.

One of the air force crewmembers said to me, "Be careful of queer men in Copacabana." Why did he say this? Perhaps he sensed I might be gay and wanted to hear my response.

Trying not to appear curious, I cautiously asked, "How will I know what they look like?"

"They wear red pants," he said.

Very interesting. Now I knew how to find gay men. Or so I thought.

I found a small hotel close to the beach in Ipanema. I was not looking for "The Girl from," but I found plenty of female prostitutes on a corner near the hotel. Or rather, they found me. With a high-pitched whistling sound they beckoned to me, but I continued walking without looking back.

The next afternoon I went to Copacabana Beach. It was June, and the weather was cool for Brazilians, but the sand was warm as I unrolled my beach towel, lay down, and waited for men in red pants—or maybe red bathing suits. To my chagrin, only pale-skinned tourists were on the beach.

I eventually rolled up my towel and walked the streets looking at shops and restaurants. I passed a young man in *gray* pants, and our eyes locked for a second. He continued walking a short distance, turned around in my direction, and stopped. I hesitated for a minute and then walked back toward him. "Do you speak English?" I asked.

"Do I speak English?" he repeated. "I have been to Jackson, Mississippi." I laughed. Of all the places in the States he visited via Greyhound bus, he named Jackson. A great pickup line, as it turned out.

After talking for a few minutes on the street, the young man, named Gilberto, invited me for a drink. As we walked down a flight of steps to the small, dark bar, I could hear someone softly playing a guitar. Other than the guitarist and the bartender, I don't remember anyone else in the bar. Talking with Gilberto was easy.

He was a law student and shared an apartment with a medical student, his childhood friend. He grew up in a poor village in Brazil's interior. His father sold timber to enable him to go to private school and then to the university in Rio.

Gilberto graduated from law school during the authoritarian military dictatorship that ruled Brazil from 1964 to 1985 and found the politics surrounding law so disgusting that he quit his practice. Eventually, he bought a jewelry store in Copacabana and a bar for his family to run. But his love was teaching English.

This chance meeting on the street in 1968 turned into a thirty-year friendship. Over the years, I returned to visit him four times, twice during Carnival, and he visited me in D.C. several times. On my last visit to Rio, I read for a class of his young students.

I think we bonded and our friendship endured because we both began to accept that we were gay in the year we met. He was my first gay friend, and we could talk about anything. I recall one conversation about the meaning of life in which he said, "Sex is the stimulant of life. You work, you fight with people, you sleep—the routine of life. What remains is nothing. You must have sex to fill the void." When he died of AIDS at the young age of fifty-two, I felt like a part of my life was lost forever. I miss him and will never forget him.

The trip to Rio unleashed my long-suppressed attraction to men, which I had been aware of from my earliest childhood memories. I was twenty-six years old and tired of hiding, but afraid that coming out of the closet would hurt my parents and destroy my military career.

When I returned to Fayetteville, I dated lots of men, a precarious situation considering the military policy that banned homosexual activities. For a year I somehow balanced working by day and dating almost every night of the week, trying to make up for lost time.

In order to help protect my identity, I assumed a fictitious name, an employee of the local telephone company. I knew that anonymous dating couldn't protect me from the potential of being identified while in uniform at Fort Bragg. Every day I saw fifteen to twenty clinical patients, and I shopped at the PX and commissary on post. The fear of being discovered was real, but didn't stop me. I had military boyfriends, and I was never caught. Lucky.

My luck continued. Soon I received orders to report to Landstuhl Army Hospital in Germany. Again, I sought housing off post, this time in the basement apartment of a German family, who lived above me. It was a charming, quiet neighborhood of single-family houses and only a five-minute drive to the hospital.

For the next twelve months I continued my duplicitous life. I dated Marsha, a chaplain's daughter, sang in the chapel choir, and was the Protestant Chapel youth leader. She moved away to go to college and two years later wrote me:

> I did have quite a hang-up on you, John. I see now that all the time I was in Europe I was looking for my "perfect match." Naturally, there were certain qualifications my ideal man was to have and I must throw roses, you had them all—as far as I could tell.

Only superficially could I have met her qualifications. Geographic distance saved us both. She ended the letter with the news that she got married "knowing it was the Lord's choice and not mine, this time!!!" I thanked God, as well.

I also dated nurses, including Lea and Sharon. I traveled with Sharon to Egypt, Cyprus, and Israel. She was beautiful, sexy, and smart. But she was not a man. Lea was a great Southern-style cook, and we had fun times together. But I continued to date men, which was potentially dangerous, because Landstuhl was a small village. People could observe comings and goings. Also, two military colleagues from the hospital lived across the street from my apartment.

During that first year in Germany, I drove from Landstuhl to other destinations in Germany, Switzerland, Austria, and France. One weekend I drove my racing-green Rover 2000 TC to Basel, where I sought out the White Horse, my first visit to a gay bar. I remember entering the small, narrow room where men were quietly talking and drinking. My stomach lurched. In my paranoia, I thought everyone turned and stared at me. I panicked and rushed out the door immediately.

Walking down the street I found a table at an outdoor café, which was perfect for people watching. A tall, thin, swarthy young man walked by my table, stopped, turned around and looked at me. His name was Abbas Zahedi, a student from Tehran. We had an instant rapport and talked about everything from Barbara Streisand's new movie, *Funny Girl*, to my yearning to find joy in life.

"I want joy and peace with God. And sex—that is the dilemma," I told Abbas.

"I don't understand. If you want joy in your life, listen to Beethoven's Ninth Symphony."

"Although I enjoy clssical music, Beethoven is not enough," I replied.

I invited Abbas to visit me in Landstuhl, and he did. That weekend's activities are blurry, but I remember I talked about Marsha at all the wrong times. I was a conflicted about my sexual feelings for him. And racked with guilt. We exchanged letters, but eventually the correspondence ended.

In 1968, I also had a brief affair with Rachael Cottingham, whom I met on a ski trip in Flims, Switzerland. We were among the seventy officers and civilians attending the weeklong Winter Sports Party, which was sponsored by the British Chapter of the Officers' Christian Union.

High in the Swiss Alps, I timidly learned to ski (mostly snowplowed) and began a romance with Rachael. In the weeks following Flims, I flew to London to see Rachael, and together we traveled by train to Sussex for a weekend with her parents. Her parents appeared to be well off and seemed to approve of me—even after I came to breakfast on Saturday morning without a jacket and tie, as did her father and brother.

Still later—I can't recall the time frame—I invited her to spend a weekend with me in Landstuhl. I remember what I tried to do, but didn't, because she stopped me and said, "You must first tell me that you love me." I could have lied and told her that I loved her. I could have made love to her, but I didn't.

The next day we were riding in my car to the train station when we heard on the radio Diana Ross and the Supremes' new hit "I'm Gonna Make You Love Me." It was only a song. I didn't lie to her. She was pretty and fun to be with, and I hoped for a future for us.

Hope was not enough; I didn't love her.

With Daniel Kane it wasn't love. It was infatuation. I met him in my clinic as a patient. After the exam he shared that he was in the process of making a decision whether to give up his French or American citizenship. (His father was American.) If he decided to retain his American citizenship, he would be subject to the military draft and could be sent to Vietnam.

Daniel invited me to visit him and his mother in Nancy, France, which I did. His mother was a lovely hostess. While touring the lovely countryside, he took me to his grandfather's abandoned farmhouse. Most of the contents had been removed, but in one of the musty rooms I noticed a sailing ship carved from wood. The two-foot-long ship was a marvel of design with sails that were intricately connected by strings. According to the carving on the hull, the ship's name was *Liberté*. His uncle who made the ship was conscripted into the military as a teenager and died during World War II. As I fingered the dusty sails of the ship, he asked me, "Do you want it?"

"Of course, I admire the ship, but it was made by your uncle," I replied.

"No one in the family wants it. It's yours."

Daniel returned with me (and the ship) to visit a few days and make a decision about his future. The days were tumultuous due to the difficult citizenship issue he faced, and the nights were sexually charged. He had difficulty dealing with gay sex and returned to Nancy. It was the last time I saw him.

While at Landstuhl, I had dated Abbas, Rachael, Daniel, Lea, Marsha, Sharon and others. I look back with regret that I was not honest or kind to these good, sweet people.

After a year, I was reassigned to a dispensary in Frankfurt. I lived in a seven-story apartment building, a fifteen-minute drive to my clinic and away from military housing. Each morning I pasted down my non-regulation, long hair with Dippity-Do hair gel, put on my uniform, and was the property of Uncle Sam for nine hours a day, Monday through Friday. But the evenings and weekends, when I was not on duty, were mine. After duty hours I combed the gel out of my hair, put on my tight-fitting bellbottom jeans, and hit the bars, freed from my military life.

In the fall of 1969, on a Saturday night in a bar in Wiesbaden, I met Karlheinz Wehhofer. We dated for a year even though I made him go out on my balcony to smoke in cold weather. I cared deeply for him.

It was difficult at first, but I accepted his announcement that he was marrying his beautiful, childhood sweetheart, Jirina. He told her about our relationship before the marriage, and she accepted me, as had Karl's parents. I was genuinely happy for Karlheinz because he could find contentment with Jirina, which I couldn't provide.

I drove from Frankfurt, Germany, to Prague for the wedding. I was anxious when I reached the German-Czech border. After all, I was an American soldier entering a Communist country. (This was years before the Velvet Revolution freed Czechoslovakia from Russian domination.) The grim border guards asked for my passport, and I was permitted to continue on. Karl, his brother, his parents, and I stayed with his grandmother in an old country house outside the city. For two days we ate copious amounts of food and consumed many bottles of wine. His grandmother prepared an excellent dumpling and goulash dish on a wood-burning stove. But it was her apple strudel, made of thin pastry and filled with fresh apples and spices, which became my future gold standard. My mouth waters as I remember the taste of the gooey apple filling and the light, flaky crust.

As we held each other close in our shared bed the night before he got married, I asked, "Are you sure of what you are doing?"

He replied, "No."

The next morning we drove into Prague for the wedding, which was held in the fourteenth-century Old Town city hall. We passed Russian soldiers in the street as we walked through the square to enter through the massive, carved, wooden Gothic door. Inside the city hall we walked up to the second floor to the registrar's office. After a brief civil ceremony, I signed their marriage license as their best man.

In December 1976, I returned to Germany to visit Karlheinz and other friends. I met him, Jirina, and their four-year-old son on a sunny, cold afternoon in a neighborhood bar. Karlheinz and Jirina were doing well—he was studying theater, and she worked for Lufthansa Airlines. Their son, Marcus John, is named after me. We had an instant rapport. Later, as we were saying our goodbyes, Marcus John asked me to spend the night with him (not unlike his father).

It was a lovely reunion, and they seemed happy. And yes, Karl said that he was sure now that he had made the right decision to get married.

The marriage lasted another year—seven in total—after I visited them in Frankfurt. But my friendship with both has remained for the forty-six years since their wedding. Karlheinz (a.k.a. Chris) became one of the two sisters in an original musical comedy cabaret that satirizes politics and the messiness of life. After more than 20 years, Chris continues his reincarnation of Anita Palmerova in the Die Bosen Schwestern traveling theater.

When Tony, my husband, and I were in Berlin in 2009, we spent a delightful Sunday in a neighborhood café with Karlheinz, Marcus John, his wife, and his children. Afterward, Marcus John, Karlheinz, Tony, and I went to a trendy bar catching up, sharing stories.

Two years later I met Jirina in Budapest for a weekend at the end of an Eastern European trip. Jirina brought her nine-year-old grandson, Karl. The three of us went to the old Ottoman-style Szechenyi baths to soak and play in the mineral water. She was just as beautiful as the first time I saw her in Prague in 1971. Although she has had boyfriends over the years, she has not remarried.

I have learned from all my relationships that no experience goes wasted, no matter the outcome. I agree with Shirley MacLaine, who said that everyone does what they do in order to learn about themselves. Some are just slow learners.

# NEVER THE SAME AGAIN

On April 1, 1973—April Fools' Day—I ended my military career by resigning my commission. Although I had avoided a court-martial for being homosexual, I could no longer live a double life. At thirty-one, I needed to grow long hair, find a long-term boyfriend, and choose a new direction for my career. While sorting out my future, I returned home for a couple of months.

Mother had a hard time accepting this unemployment period while I was exploring future plans. My parents had financed the majority of my college and optometry school education and were worried about my future. I think she was embarrassed when neighbors and family asked her, "What is Carroll doing? Where is he working?"

During the months I lived at home I was usually in a pensive mood. Quiet. Not fun to be around. She sensed I was in turmoil—as mothers do—and said, "Carroll, you have changed. You are not the same." Of course, she was right.

The year 1973 was momentous. Not only did I leave the military, but I also decided to tell my parents that I was gay. Earlier in the year the American Psychiatric Association declassified homosexuality as a disease. Imagine that: I was diseased and now I'm not. The APA's policy change gave added motivation for me to come out.

It was a summer evening, and the three of us were watching *Bell, Book and Candle* on TV. The movie starred Kim Kovak, who was rumored to be lesbian. I took this moment as a sign that the time to tell was now. I turned to my parents and said, "I have something important to tell you. I am gay."

"J, turn off the TV," Mother said.

I had been rehearsing all the right words to use: I have always been attracted to men; this was not a phase; I had prayed to God to change me; I was tired of lying; I was afraid they would no longer love me. The words tumbled out, and the conversation was tense and tearful. I tried to respond to their concerns that they had done something wrong to make this happen. I told them it was no one's fault; being gay is not a fault. I knew that my sexuality was difficult for them to accept because of their religious beliefs and fears of what the family and neighbors would say. At the end of this painful conversation, Daddy said, "We don't understand this, but we love you, son."

My parents didn't kick me out of the house for being gay, as happens with some children. But living in my parents' attic was a temporary arrangement, and I needed to move on with my life. I chose Chapel Hill, because I heard it was a liberal town with a gay community, and I wanted to live a halcyon life, completely out of the closet.

I rented a secluded place at the end of a paved road. I loved the fresh spring water pumped into the house. I planted a small garden. Although I lived in the country, it only took me 15 minutes to drive to Chapel Hill. I didn't know anyone, so as a way to meet new people, I auditioned and won roles in a couple of amateur theater productions, including a singing mock turtle in *Alice's Adventures Underground*. (I channeled the voice of Paul Lynde.) My thespian avocation continued.

While in Chapel Hill, I had three special boyfriends—each relationship lasted about a year. Michael Kenna was beginning his senior year at Duke when we met. He was intelligent, artistic, and fun. I remember our daytime romp in Duke Forest, his dance performance to the sound of humpback whales at the east campus theatre, and his encouraging me to play my accordion on a sunny Sunday afternoon on the lush, south lawn of the historic Sarah P. Duke Gardens. I played the Duke gig accompanied by the contemporary dance of Susan White. People leisurely walking by mostly ignored us.

In May I attended Michael's graduation, which was distinctive in that Canadian Prime Minister Pierre Elliott Trudeau (whose son is the current PM) was the honored speaker. Graduation marked the end of our relationship because Michael was ready to move to San Francisco to write the first great gay novel; but, sadly, he died of AIDS at age forty without writing a novel.

I enjoyed my amateur acting, sleeping late, watching old TV movie classics, going out every single night, and frequently dancing at a local club, the Electric Company. But it was time to make a decision about future employment.

I never forgot while growing up in rural North Carolina that no one in our community had health insurance. My parents and neighbors worked for minimum wage with no benefits. Daddy *always* tithed 10 percent of his meager income, and I don't know how they afforded doctor visits. I was a sickly child and instead of taking me to a doctor, I remember on more than one occasion my parents, in an effort to save money, took me in the evening to the home of a nurse for a shot of penicillin. (In the 1950s, penicillin was a miracle drug.) While waiting for her to fill the syringe, I saw the needles in a pot on her kitchen stove. The needles had been boiled, not autoclaved or disposed of after use. After one of these injections, I developed a fever and the white of my eyes turned yellow: I had contracted hepatitis from the contaminated needles.

Memories of my childhood experiences in accessing affordable health care and my interest in politics and government policy led me to enroll in the University of North Carolina's School of Public Health master's program in health administration. I wanted to go to Washington with a degree in health administration, to be part of new government policies to address our country's health care system. I believed (and still do) that it is a moral imperative to provide affordable health care for everyone.

I could have finished the program in one year with a full load of courses, but I stretched it out for two years because for the first time in my life I enjoyed being a student. I was openly gay, which was no big deal for the other students or faculty. Being out of the closet also removed an invisible barrier, which enabled me to learn effectively in small work groups, as well as the classroom. I could speak and not be concerned about being perceived as gay. It was a non-issue.

One of the most popular freshman courses was Human Sexuality 101. I was selected to be a facilitator for small work group discussions, which augmented the large class lectures. As an openly gay man, it was liberating talking to these students about my own sexuality.

In 1974, I became one of the founding members of the University of North Carolina's Carolina Gay Association (CGA), which was eventually recognized as an official student group. Our monthly meetings, which were held in the Student Union Building, made a visible statement that we were part of campus life. The friends I made at CGA became my kith—my inner circle—and a few remain my friends to this day.

To dispel misinformation and the odium about gay people, I enthusiastically became a member of our speakers' group, which went to classes at UNC and other universities to tell our stories and answer questions. (At that time, gay men and lesbians were an exotic and maligned species.) I also got a kick out of being the DJ for CGA's monthly dances. I packed up my own disco records, phono player and speakers, and set them up in Craig Hall on campus. Our dance night was open to gay and straight students—a revolutionary concept for a North Carolina university.

The CGA was the catalyst for advocacy for gay rights—I believe to help make up for those years of suppression in the military. Realizing my own struggles, I wanted to make it easier for gay students to come out and for others to accept their gay friends and relatives.

During my second year at Chapel Hill, I met John Adams. John had longish, brown hair, wore big glasses and loved to sing in a madrigal group. We shared a house and a similar conservative religious upbringing. Some months into our relationship, we went to rural Pennsylvania for a weekend with his parents, without any untoward incidents. Eventually, I brought John home for a weekend with my parents. Since we were there on a Sunday, we went to church. There in the church narthex I introduced John to my grandpa "Pop" Whitener. He took one look at John, and without pausing, asked me, "Is this your new girlfriend?"

I didn't have a rejoinder and changed the subject. Pop, who was illiterate, spent his childhood in the fields, not attending school. But he was no one's fool. Who was I kidding? But I mostly honored my parents' request to not tell my extended family that I was gay. My parents' problem was they couldn't handle the imagined responses of my relatives. On several occasions mother expressed her fear that someone in Hickory would find out I was gay, which would be devastating to her.

During my third year in Chapel Hill I met sweet, quiet Charles Faison. After bringing him home for a weekend, mother asked me not to bring any more boyfriends home. She said, "I can't take it." Painful words. In her mind, I was living in sin manifest by sleeping with my boyfriend in her house. I got it.

Charles and I shared my secluded house in the country, while he attended the UNC School of Pharmacy, and I finished my master's degree. My fondest memory of us is walking hand-in-hand across the UNC campus. There were no verbal or physical attacks. This simple, heartfelt action was liberating.

For my field project, I spent the summer of 1976 with the Phoenix Indian Medical Center. I provided eye care with an ophthalmologist to remote Native American sites in Arizona. The expedient way to reach the reservations was by using a small two-engine plane. It was my first experience with the effect of desert heat while flying. Periodically, the plane forcefully bounced up and down while in flight, but we safely landed. Mission complete.

In spite of the fiery heat, I ventured out for two exceptionally different weekends—Las Vegas (unnatural blemish on the desert) and the Grand Canyon (spectacular wonder of the world). My friend Neil and I walked down the south rim some 4,000 feet to the Havasupai reservation and camped overnight by a cool, clear, blue-green stream. The next morning the sound of Native American children playing in the river awakened us. Later as we headed back up the canyon, I thought I would die in the stifling August heat. Buzzards circled overhead.

The buzzards must have been an omen, because when I returned to Chapel Hill a few weeks later, the relationship with Charles was over. Over the summer, he realized that he wanted to live his life without me. His departure was painful, because I still cared for him.

It turns out that networking with Indian Health Service optometrists while in Phoenix, resulted in an invitation to serve on the American Optometric Association's (AOA) task force examining access to eye care services. From the task force meetings, I met David Lewis, who offered me a job interview. I borrowed a suit from my friend Martin Less and went to Washington, where I had a successful interview. At the age of 35 and with no professional political experience, I landed a job as AOA's Assistant Director for Public Health in Government Relations.

I was clear with AOA from the beginning that I was gay: I was not going to hide my identity from another employer. At my first office Christmas party, I brought my date, Ricky Rankin. No eyes rolled, no heads turned.

It was a heady, hopeful time for potential health care reform. Jimmy Carter had been elected President, promising reform with universal national health insurance. Carter, who grew up in rural America, the son of a nurse, knew firsthand about poor people and their lack of healthcare. Carter wanted a role for private insurance but also proposed to expand Medicaid coverage. He became embroiled in a bitter fight with Senator Kennedy, who wanted to phase in comprehensive coverage by a single-payer system, like Medicare, with individual and employer mandates. Kennedy withdrew support of the resulting compromised health bill, and it died in 1980.

I was sorely disappointed when the health care reform bill died. I obtained a degree in health administration and went to D.C. to help change our country's health care policy. I believed then, as I do now, that health care is a right, not a privilege.

Martin Less and I became good friends while at Chapel Hill in the public health master's program. Later, when he expressed interest in moving to the D.C. area to work, I invited him to stay with me. We were compatible housemates so we decided to buy a house together in south Arlington. Martin became involved in Bet Mishpachah, a congregation for gay and lesbian Jews. I was taking a hiatus from volunteering for any gay organization. One day he said, "John, it's time for you to get back into working with a gay rights group." He was right.

I read in the *Washington Blade* newspaper about the Arlington Gay and Lesbian Association (AGLA) in Arlington, Virginia. I attended meetings and worked on projects, and in 1984 I became the group's president. While I was president, I organized the first meeting with three state house representatives and members of AGLA, which was the beginning of an annual Democratic candidates' forums (Republican candidates declined invitation). I worked with the lesbian ex-wife of a policeman to establish a liaison between AGLA and the local police department, resulting in sensitivity training to improve relations between the police and the gay community. I also initiated AGLA's official participation in laying a wreath at the Tomb of the Unknowns on Veterans Day. This ceremony was bittersweet as we recognized gay and lesbian soldiers who had died for our country, but whose country denied them the freedom of being openly gay.

As many of my friends became sick and died, my interest in AIDS education and access to services extended beyond public health and became personal. With the increasing threat of AIDS, the Arlington County manager created a special AIDS Task Force. I was appointed to this task force, which produced a long-range plan to address AIDS education and services within the county. I served on the board and became chair of the Whitman Walker Clinic of Northern Virginia. The clinic was a satellite office of the Whitman Walker Clinic in D.C., which initially provided HIV testing and counseling services, for gay men, eventually expanding to include medical, dental, and other health care services for all patients.

By simply asking, I was appointed to the Arlington County Schools Health and Physical Education Committee and served for seven years. During that time I successfully advocated for staff to create an AIDS education curriculum for the Arlington school system, which included lesson plans for kindergarten through twelfth grade. I reviewed and recommended textbooks with positive or neutral information about homosexuality. At this time most textbooks contained only negative statements. I championed study plans that included factual information about homosexuality in the school system's sex education curriculum.

The fight for a new sex education curriculum that presented factual information about homosexuality was an ugly, tough battle. Teaching sex education in schools—especially when the subject is homosexuality—brought out crazy, homophobic people at public forums.

During one of our Health and Physical Education meetings the discussion strayed to religious beliefs and objections to homosexuality. I had been quietly lobbying Peggy Fisher—who at first sight could appear to be anyone's sweet, gray-haired grandmother—to advocate for adding factual information about homosexuality to the curriculum. Peggy said that bringing church teachings into the classroom was inappropriate policy. Our committee had a particularly offensive member, who turned to Peggy and disdainfully said, "You must be a Unitarian." Defiantly, Peggy responded, "Yes, I am."

Another night after a particularly partisan, name-calling meeting, I returned to my home and called my parents seeking solace. I broke down and cried as I recalled the vicious remarks made by people at the meeting. Daddy calmly reminded me that people could be ugly to us, but God was still on his throne (Psalm 11:4) and loved me. For that moment Daddy, the wise and loving parent, overcame his judgment of me as a sinner. I found peace in his words.

# TIME HEALS EVERYTHING

At a family gathering in the early eighties, my cousin Barry asked, "Why don't you join the Army Reserve and get credit for your years of active duty towards a twenty-year retirement?" Barry had entered the army about the same time as I, and after his tour was complete, he joined the Army Reserve.

I could have said, "Because it is illegal to be a gay person in the Army Reserve." Instead I replied, "I will think about it."

For most of my life I had learned how to keep quiet about being gay and live with the rules, including my eight-and-a-half years on active duty. Now I was openly gay at my civilian job and in every aspect of my life. How did I think I could remain closeted in the Army Reserve? Because I knew how to compartmentalize my life.

In 1982—at the age of forty—I joined the Army Reserve to serve two days each month and two weeks each year at Walter Reed Army Hospital, in Washington, D.C. I could handle being part-time military, and my sexuality had nothing to do with the quality of military service. But why did I rejoin an organization that didn't want me and could kick me out, if they knew I was gay? Why risk the humiliation? Why subject myself to oppressive, discriminatory military rules?

I still can't fully rationalize my actions, but I raised my hand and swore to defend the Constitution against all enemies as an Army Reserve officer. I enjoyed examining patients at Walter Reed Army Hospital surrounded my colleagues from India, Romania, Haiti, and all over the U.S.A. I admit that on some level I enjoyed defying the rules and getting by with it. I was also trying to disprove the stereotype of a gay man being unmanly, unfit to be a soldier. Perhaps all the reasons I gave for rejoining the Army still didn't add up. Perhaps I was a closeted patriot, who loved his country—and his country's men.

My colleagues in our hospital unit were not macho men. (Of course, it helped that about half were female.) Over the years, if anyone suspected I was gay, I never knew it: They didn't ask, and I didn't tell. I never heard anyone discussing homosexuality, even when a well-liked enlisted soldier in our unit was diagnosed with AIDS. It was a non-issue.

During the two weeks at summer training (the extra money was useful), I carried my weight and contributed my skills, as did my colleagues. Over the years, I received two Army Commendation Medals for meritorious performance of duties during summer training camps and an Army Achievement Medal for exceptionally meritorious service during Operation Desert Storm.

Two years after joining the unit, I was promoted to major in a ceremony in front of my colleagues. The commanding hospital general, whose name I have forgotten, pinned the gold oak leaf on my uniform. I was proud of my achievement. I threw a "Major Party" at my house in Arlington and invited only my gay friends. I continued to compartmentalize my life.

In 1984, I met Tony Saldana the old-fashioned way—a personal ad in the *Washington Blade*: "Wanted a Latin man, thirty years or older, for long-term relationship." Five people answered the ad, but I like to say that Tony was the winner. Our first date was at a Hungarian pastry shop in Dupont Circle. After two years of dating, we moved into a house in south Arlington.

In 2008, while on a vacation to British Columbia, Tony and I were married. Although it was the twenty-fourth anniversary of our relationship, our wedding was a serendipitous happening.

We stayed at a bed-and-breakfast, which was a picturesque golden yellow Victorian with forest-green trim and hanging baskets of geraniums and petunias on the wraparound open-air porch. Our rooms were in a small cottage with a path to the front door lined with white, yellow, and pink blooming rose bushes.

Our second day during breakfast in their formal dining room, I casually asked Fernando and Don, the gay couple who owned the guesthouse, how to get married in Victoria.

"Walk three blocks to Robson Street to the Vital Statistics Agency office located in the bank building. Take your passports and pay a hundred-dollar license fee," said Don. "You can have the civil ceremony in our parlor, and we can be your witnesses."

"Wow. Is it that simple?" I asked. "How civilized."

"We have a friend, Laurie Smith, who is a marriage commissioner. She can conduct the ceremony and make it official," said Fernando. The night before we were married, Ms. Smith called us and asked what we wanted read at the marriage ceremony.

"Short and sweet," Tony and I said almost simultaneously.

The next day the Marriage Commissioner read the following:

> We come together here today to witness the joining in the state of matrimony of John and Antonio according to the order and the custom prevailing and under the authority that has been given and provided by the Government of the Province of British Columbia.
>
> Marriage, as we understand it, is a state that has been ennobled and enriched by a long and honorable tradition of devotion. It is set in the basis of the law of our land, affording each of the two participants equality before that law, and supporting the common rights of each of the two individuals in this marriage.
>
> You have a desire for a lifelong companionship with the generous sharing of the help and the comfort that a married couple ought to have from one another, through

whatever circumstance of joy and sorrow, sickness or health, adversity or prosperity that your lives may experience.

Marriage is, therefore, not to be entered upon thoughtlessly or irresponsibly, but, instead, with a due and serious understanding, an appreciation of the ends for which it was begun, and of the material, the intellectual, and the emotional factors which will contribute to its fulfillment. A marriage, by its very nature, is a state of giving, of offering, for a marriage requires the giving of one's self, in order to support the marriage and the home in which it may flourish.

The Commissioner continued:

Do you, John, promise to give to Antonio, the love of your person, the comfort of your companionship, and the patience of your understanding? Do you promise to share equally with him of the necessities of life? Do you promise to respect the dignity of his person with his own personal rights? And finally, do you promise to recognize the need for open communication on all matters that pertain either to the present or to the future of this household that you are creating today with your marriage to Antonio.

I answered, "I do."

The brief ceremony was lovely. Tony selected the music, which played during the ceremony: *Marche Pour la Ceremonie des Turcs* by Jean Baptiste Lully, *Sonnerie de Ste Genevieve du Mont de Paris* by Marin Marais, and *Convento di Sant'anna* by Gabriel Yared.

Two weeks later we received the official marriage license in the mail.

In 2014, following the landmark Supreme Court decision, a federal judge in North Carolina struck down the state's same-sex marriage ban*, which made our Canadian marriage legal in North Carolina and all states. After thirty years together, without the benefit of a legal marriage, our commitment was finally recognized,

* Ironically, the same year Vietnam's National Assembly struck down the ban on same sex marriage. At that time, the American ambassador to Vietnam, Ted Osius, was openly gay and lived with his husband and two adopted children.

our relationship was validated!

The following month we had a private ceremony at my church, First Congregational United Church of Christ, where we renewed our marriage vows and our minister blessed our marriage. Tony and I promised each other to be "an entity for eternity," and that is a long, long time. My parents set the example: They were married 71 years.

While growing up, I dreamed of a successful marriage and career. In my youth, marriage to a man was out of the question, but that changed. At the age of thirty-three, I wasn't confident about changing my vocation to public health, but I did. As for my career, I believe I made a difference in national policy that improved access to vision care services. I am hopeful that future administrations will continue to provide funding for millions of people who otherwise could not afford health care.

In 2008, I was awarded an honorary degree by the Illinois College of Optometry for lifetime contributions to improve public health. I delivered the commencement address in the stunning, gothic Rockefeller Chapel on the Campus of the University of Chicago. But my speech paled compared to the pageantry of walking down the long aisle to the lectern of the chapel engulfed in the distinctive sound of bagpipes played by men in kilts.

In 2013, I received another honorary doctorate degree and delivered the commencement address at the New England College of Optometry in Boston. In my speech I acknowledged that this day was not about me, but about the graduates, their families, and friends. Using three real-life stories, I challenged the new graduates to get involved in community health programs, health policy, and politics—all within a 10-minute speech.

Tony was treated as my husband at both commencements and the honorary dinners. The recognition by my peers at two colleges was the capstone to my long career in public health and policy in Washington. After 30 years, it was time to retire.

For nearly a decade, I honored my mother's request to not bring another boyfriend home. With Tony, I finally broke the rule. After meeting Tony and liking him, my parents eventually began to visit us in our home for the ten years we lived in Arlington. They spent Christmas with us for many of those years, and their visits to our home continued when we moved to Asheville. My parents never approved of my sexuality, yet on some level there was acceptance of Tony. In their eyes, I believe, we were not married; therefore, Tony was not my legitimate spouse. This became apparent to me at Christmas, when Mother bought gifts for the spouses of my siblings, but not for Tony. Although this was painful, I didn't speak to my mother about it. Also, I didn't tell them about our marriage in Canada, and they didn't live to see the Supreme Court ruling that legalized gay and lesbian marriages.

After the Supreme Court had legalized marriage equality, I was ready to ask for recognition with the military. I called the local National Guard Armory to make an appointment for Tony to have his photo made for his military-dependent ID card to use for spousal benefits. I talked with a sergeant who told me that my spouse would need to bring a birth certificate, driver's license, social security card, and marriage license. After telling him that my *husband* and I were married in Canada, I expected pushback, but to my surprise, he responded, "I have never had someone show an out-of-country marriage license." His voice revealed no judgment or disapproval. He made the appointment for the ID card and said if I didn't hear back from him, everything was a go.

Two weeks later at the appointed time a young man at the National Guard Armory called us into his office and asked for Tony's papers. As he was entering the information into his computer, he asked, "What day and year were you married?" There was a delay in our response as we were trying to remember the exact date. With a smile on his face he said, "Who will be first to remember the date?"

The process was quick and professional. After the young man gave Tony his new military-dependent ID card, he shook his hand and said, "Congratulations." With his new card Tony was now entitled to military health care and other benefits, previously denied. We both cried as we walked out to the parking lot. I had lived long enough to see the U.S. military recognize our marriage—and my husband. I felt that at last my military career was legitimate.

Mother was right: I was not the same person after Vietnam. My faith has changed and grown since those difficult days of questioning. I still question, and I don't have all the answers to the mysteries of God, but I no longer wonder if God loves me as I am. I no longer fear that my sexuality and spirituality are incompatible. I am who God created me to be. It just took me too long to accept that truth.

Mick Jagger was right. Time has been on my side, after all. I have lived to witness monumental changes in antigay laws, beginning with the 2003 Supreme Court decision overturning state sodomy laws and continuing with the 2014 decision that recognized gay marriages. Unlike the beginning of my military career, gay people can now serve openly and proudly in the military.

Although I am grateful for the massive shift in people's acceptance of gay friends, family, and neighbors, discrimination remains in federal and state laws. Employers in 28 states can fire people for being gay. Since the 1990s when it was first introduced, Congress has failed to pass the Employment Nondiscrimination Act, which would protect gay people in the workplace.

Although the Supreme Court has ruled that laws to enforce sexual conduct between consenting adults are unconstitutional, North Carolina and eight other states still maintain Crime Against Nature statutes, which historically have been used to prosecute homosexual sex. It is offensive for the statues to remain in state law, which are a vivid reminder of a shameful time in history not so many years ago.

The struggle for gay, lesbian and transgender people's equal rights continues. After my generation dies off, I believe that society will be even more inclusive, and gay people will be perceived as no more intrinsically evil or virtuous than heterosexual people.

Since I came out to my parents almost forty years ago, Daddy and I had many heated, enraged exchanges about my sexuality. Over the years we had equally inflamed discussions about abortion. I called a halt to these discussions; neither of us was ever going to change our viewpoints.

Regardless of our disagreements, I am grateful that my Daddy was a hugger, an emotional person, who seldom held back his tears. After a visit, he would tear up as he hugged me goodbye. I never once doubted that he loved me, but his religious beliefs never allowed him to accept my sexuality. He based his beliefs on a strict, fundamentalist interpretation of the Bible. He read it cover-to-cover more than once.

During the last year of Daddy's life, I remember sitting down in the living room with him after I spent an exhausting day in hospice with Mother. We talked about the events of the day, nothing noteworthy. After a lull in the conversation, he turned to me and said, "Son, I am proud of you."

I am eternally thankful for these six words.

# ACKNOWLEDGEMENTS

I wish to express heartfelt thanks to the following:

For invaluable editing by Penny Stokes, who was there for me in the beginning and helped me focus my writing; and Karen Richardson Dunn, who encouraged me to dig deep into my emotions and expand the stories.

For significant review and suggested changes to the manuscript: Devon Corley (my young gay eyes), Don Pfister (my grand inquisitor), Nancie McDermott (fabulous cook and storyteller) and Dean Nichols (the best dresser in the world).

For offering their advice and encouragement: John Crocker, Ilene Kasper, David Haltiwanger and Tony Saldana.

For artistic design and layout: Robert Bradley.

Made in the USA
Middletown, DE
18 November 2017

SEP 2018